CHILDHOOD SEXUAL ABUSE

BELIEVING VICTIMS AND SUPPORTING SURVIVORS

Why Do We Do So Little When We Know So Much?

DR. DEBORAH INMAN

CHILDHOOD SEXUAL ABUSE: BELIEVING VICTIMS AND SUPPORTING SURVIVORS WHY DO WE DO SO LITTLE WHEN WE KNOW SO MUCH?

iUniverse books may be ordered through booksellers or by contacting:

iUniverse
1663 Liberty Drive
Bloomington, IN 47403
www.iuniverse.com
1-800-Authors (1-800-288-4677)

Because of the dynamic nature of the Internet, any web addresses or links contained in this book may have changed since publication and may no longer be valid. The views expressed in this work are solely those of the author and do not necessarily reflect the views of the publisher, and the publisher hereby disclaims any responsibility for them.

Any people depicted in stock imagery provided by Getty Images are models, and such images are being used for illustrative purposes only. Certain stock imagery © Getty Images.

ISBN: 978-1-5320-5495-2 (sc)
ISBN: 978-1-5320-5497-6 (hc)
ISBN: 978-1-5320-5496-9 (e)

Library of Congress Control Number: 2018909701

Print information available on the last page.

iUniverse rev. date: 08/13/2018

To all survivors of childhood sexual abuse
and to the families who support them

Contents

Preface

In 2017, many women broke their silence and came forward to accuse the powerful men who had sexually abused them and to demand they be held accountable for their crimes. This resulted in the reappearance of the #MeToo movement, which originated with Tarana Burke in 2006 and was reignited by Alyssa Milano in 2017 when she posted to social media and asked anyone who had been a victim of sexual abuse to respond with #MeToo, to provide a sense of the magnitude of the problem. This has brought long overdue attention to the inappropriate and criminal behavior suffered by many women and men who were sexually abused by people who had power over them in some way. The #MeToo movement has united many victims of sexual abuse and empowered them to come forward. While this movement has many people from the entertainment arena speaking out, others are also coming forward, including photographers, models, government officials, and even young girls training for the Olympics who were sexually abused by their sports doctor.

Previously, sexual abuse has been overlooked or removed from the spotlight after reaching the height of media attention with public figures like Sandusky, Catholic priests, Boy Scout leaders, and others who have power over children. However, the current #MeToo movement has kept the media coverage going and has resulted in penalties for those who have been identified as the perpetrators.

Although many are speaking out through the #MeToo movement, survivors of childhood sexual abuse are less likely to come forward if they are not part of a larger group speaking out, especially if they are the victims of incest. While #MeToo may be helpful for adults, it is less likely that children who are victims of sexual abuse will come forward. Children are the silent majority of victims of sexual predators and pedophiles. This book is a call for true justice to protect and support survivors of childhood sexual abuse.

Introduction

The purpose of this book is to raise awareness of the need to believe, support, and improve the lives of survivors of childhood sexual abuse and to call for stronger policies and a more just legal system to protect and support victims/survivors and hold abusers accountable for their actions, regardless of the age of the child.

Despite increasing publicity regarding high-profile cases, the details of childhood sexual abuse remain difficult to discuss for victims and their families. Childhood sexual abuse is considered one of the most heinous crimes and continues to be underreported. The children who are victims are powerless to their abusers. The word of the child is often doubted, and many of these abused children go through life without any support or understanding of the actual impact of this abuse on their ability to develop healthy and productive life experiences.

These children depend on the legal system to protect them. However, the system often does not work, and this is an even greater injustice. The system promises to protect and punish, but in many cases of childhood sexual abuse, this promise is broken, so the children suffer even more, knowing their offender is not being held accountable for the heinous crime. As these children try to move forward with life, they experience post-traumatic stress disorder (PTSD), eating disorders, mental health issues, addictions, learning difficulties, and many other life challenges. Most have no support services to help them get through life, as they are surviving day to day. Moreover, the nonabusive parent has little support and lacks the knowledge and understanding of how this abuse will impact the child's life.

The sexual assault allegations made in the fall of 2017 and continuing into 2018, by successful women against powerful men, along with the #Me Too movement that has resulted in many other women coming forward, opened the door to calls for a movement for *all* sexual abuse victims, including children. With this movement comes a call for true justice and needed changes in policies to protect and support survivors of childhood sexual abuse.

It is time to help the many survivors of childhood sexual abuse. The pain, anguish, and shattered dreams of so many individuals cannot be left unresolved and forgotten. For those abused by a parent or someone they loved and trusted, this unforgiveable, heinous act can cause trauma and issues throughout the child's life. This book provides information and specific resources to help all parents be more aware of what they need to know about childhood sexual abuse. Further, the purpose of this book is to increase awareness of how decisions are made every day "in the best interest of the child" when children have been sexually abused and how these decisions impact the lives of these children and their families.

Questions to Consider

- Are decisions made in the best interest of the child for that moment in time or for a lifetime?
- How will the decisions in the best interest of the child impact the family? How will they affect the economic and social aspects of the family?
- What criteria are used to make these decisions?
- Are the nonabusive parents prepared for the reality of how their lives will change as a result of this experience?
- Are the nonabusive parents informed of what to expect regarding the impact of the abuse on the child in later years?
- Are the parents informed about future emotional and psychological issues?
- Are parents provided information regarding signs and symptoms to look for that might suggest their child is suffering in later years from this earlier trauma?
- Do the parents understand that the child/family may suffer PTSD?
- Are therapy sessions and the costs associated with that included in any remedies?
- Are foregone earnings discussed as a concern related to PTSD?
- What role do attorneys and the legal system play?
- What role do psychologists/therapists in the mental health professional field play in the lives of these families?

- What support should be provided to the child victims who struggle to survive every day because of post-traumatic stress disorder from this experience?
- Are children protected from pedophiles and sex abusers who are not prosecuted and are not on a sex offender list, and therefore free to continue their heinous crimes?

This book includes information based on current research and statistics as well as true legal cases of child abuse victims who are survivors and whose lives were determined by the decisions of the courts. Questions are raised regarding if indeed these decisions were in the best interest of the child, and documentation is provided as to why child survivors feel no justice was served. Further, the lifelong health consequences of these children are identified to document the need for broader long-term support for sexually abused children.

The information in this book is presented by topics and divided into chapters in an effort to help *all* parents understand what they need to know about childhood sexual abuse.

Chapter 1 documents the pervasiveness of childhood sexual abuse in the United States and provides statistics regarding the many victims and survivors of this heinous crime.

Chapter 2 provides information and resources for parents to help them better understand the prevalence of childhood sexual abuse and what to do to protect and support their children.

Chapter 3 provides information to help parents and mental health professionals including psychologists/therapists understand how the child might feel after telling their secret about what happened to them.

Chapter 4 documents how a parent's life is impacted if their child is sexually abused and provides information to support parents during this time.

Chapter 5 provides information useful to parents of children who do come forward to tell about their abuse, to help the child begin the healing process as soon as possible. Because most survivors of childhood sexual abuse do not come forward to speak about this until they are adults, there is not much information available from the perspectives of survivors who speak to the real experiences of childhood, adolescence and into early adulthood. This chapter is especially helpful to guide parents and therapists through the process of helping victims/survivors who are trying to deal with this throughout their childhood, adolescence, and into adulthood.

Chapter 6 provides a detailed examination of a true legal case of children who were sexually abused during their preschool years and the impact of that abuse throughout their childhood, adolescence, and early adult years. These experiences were a result of the sexual abuse as well as the decisions made in the best interest of the child by the courts at that time.

Chapter 7 is a call to action for policy makers, the legal profession, and mental health professionals, to step up and hold all sexual abusers accountable for their heinous crimes against children.

CHAPTER 1

Childhood Sexual Abuse: The Realities of the Problem

Children are the silent majority of victims of pedophiles and sexual predators. Ninety percent of childhood sexual abuse victims are abused by family members and trusted adults. These perpetrators are not strangers, and the children have lifelong mental health issues because of the breach of trust by a parent, family member or trusted adult committing this heinous crime. It is critical to raise awareness and understanding within and across communities, cities, states, and the nation about the extent of childhood sexual abuse and the needs of these survivors.

All survivors of childhood sexual abuse deserve the right

- to be heard,
- to be believed,
- to hold their abusers accountable, and
- to receive any needed mental health and other support services.

Childhood sexual abuse continues to be one of the most difficult topics to understand, with a perceived stigma still attached to those victims, resulting in continued injustice for the victims and survivors. We need a more just legal system to protect and support victims, along with improved decisions regarding the best interest of the child, including long-term support for survivors' mental health and other needs.

Childhood Sexual Abuse Statistics

Reports of childhood sexual abuse are on the rise. However, these reports represent a small percentage of the actual incidents of sexual abuse because so many are not reported. Seventy-three percent of child victims do not tell anyone about the abuse for at least a year. Forty-five percent of victims do not tell anyone for at least five years. Some victims never tell (Smith et al. 2000; Broman-Fulks et al. 2007; RAINN, 2018, Darkness to Light, 2018).

It is important to note that in 96 to 98 percent of child abuse cases that are reported to officials, the children's statements were found to be true (NSW Child Protection Council 1998; U.S. Department of Health and Human Services, 2013, 2014). However, studies have shown that only one in three adults would believe a child if they said they were victims of sexual abuse (Australian Childhood Foundation 2010; RAINN, 2018). This suggest that many children who do tell are not believed, are not removed from the abuser, and are not provided the support needed as a result of this abuse.

Individuals and families of all races, religions, incomes, professions, levels of education, and class are equally affected by childhood sexual abuse and incest. Alarmingly, a significant number of these children are abused before the age of 10. Approximately, one third of all children are sexually abused before the age of 18, including 40% of all girls and 30% of all boys. (The American Academy of Experts on Traumatic Stress, Bogorad 1998; U.S. Department of Health and Human Services, 2013, 2014). Ninety percent of child sexual abuse victims are abused by family members and other trusted adults, including clergy and teachers. The statistics regarding this heinous crime are staggering and are provided below.

In the United States there are more than sixty million survivors of sexual abuse, and of these, forty million survivors are under the age of thirteen (Merryn 2004, 2012). Every eight minutes, Child Protective Services substantiates or finds evidence for a claim of childhood sexual abuse; this is just from those reported (RAINN, 2018). It is important to note that most childhood sexual abuse is not reported, so the actual number of victims is much higher. Unless changes are made in our legal system, another 400,000 children who are born in the United States each year will become victims of childhood sexual abuse (Townsend and Rheingold 2013). Further, at least 325,000 children are at risk of becoming victims of commercial child sexual exploitation each year.

To put this in perspective, the statistics provided below from Darkness to Light (2018) and RAINN (2018) confirm the following information.

How many children are sexually abused?

- 1 in 10 children will be sexually abused before age 18

Girls:
- 1 in 7 girls will be sexually abused before age 18
- 12.3% of girls are age 10 or younger when first abused
- 30% of girls are between the ages of 11 and 17

Boys:
- 1 in 25 boys will be sexually abused before age 18
- 27.8% of boys are age 10 or younger when first abused
- Of all children who are sexually abused, both girls and boys:
  - 60% will never talk about it
  - 93% will know their abusers
  - 34% are under age 12
  - 66% are age 12–17

Who abuses children?

o 34% of people who sexually abuse a child are family members

o 80% of perpetrators are a parent of the child

o 50% of those who abuse children under the age of 6 are parents

o 6% of the abusers are other relatives

o 4% of the abusers are unmarried partners of a parent

o 59% of perpetrators are acquaintances, including clergy and teachers

o 7% of the abusers are strangers

o 88% of people who sexually abuse children are male

o 9% of the abusers are female

o 76.8% of people who sexually abuse children are adults

Sources: www.rainn.org/statistics/children-and-teens (2018) and www.d2l.org (2018).

Why Do We Do So Little When We Know So Much?

Although current rhetoric suggests childhood sexual abuse is no longer a taboo topic, the reality is it may not be taboo among those who work with abused children, or in organizations trying to raise awareness, but for much of society at large, including friends, family, employers, neighbors, and others in the community, this heinous crime remains a taboo topic. Many people are not comfortable discussing the topic of childhood sexual abuse, and nonoffending parents and victims feel they may be judged. Many do not recognize that the nonabusive parent is also a victim, has suffered PTSD, and has difficulty knowing how to move forward to support the child. So the nonoffending parent also needs support.

As mentioned earlier, decisions are made every day by parents, lawyers, teachers, priests, judges, and community and political entities regarding "the best interest of the child." One of the most difficult topics for anyone, including educators, psychologists, medical doctors, legal entities, and various coalitions, is the sexual abuse of children. It is considered one of the most heinous and underreported crimes against children who are victims to people they trust.

When they are reported, the legal system seldom supports the child, because of the design of our legal system. It is built on the premise that the defendant is presumed innocent, which suggests the victim is lying. Rosenbaum (2005, 2013) has identified the disparities between what citizens expect and what they experience from our legal system through court decisions. Further, he documents the inequities and the injustice of our legal system. Rosenbaum (2005, 2013) challenges the law as it is written and executed with the expectation of justice and what is and is not rendered through our justice system. Rosenbaum's concern about why our legal system fails to do what is right relates directly to child abuse. These human rights violations affect children and families of every race, religion, education, income, and profession.

Social Justice and Social Change

The children who are victims are powerless to their abusers. The victims are afraid to tell anyone what is happening to them because they are threatened. The word of the child is often doubted, and many of these abused children go through life without any support or understanding of the actual impact of this abuse on their ability to develop healthy and productive life experiences. Our legal system supports the perpetrator, presuming their innocence over the validity of the accusations of a child. Thus, that child is never given a chance for justice or healing after such a devastating experience, and the accused goes on to commit more heinous crimes against more children who will suffer the same injustice.

Social change needs to occur in this area. Too many children (and families) are victims; they suffer in silence and never receive the justice they deserve. Nor do they receive the resources and support needed to function successfully in life.

The Challenges of Coming Forward after Being Sexually Abused

A story never told is forgotten because others never even know it happened. Many children who suffer childhood sexual abuse never tell their stories because of fear.

With the recent events of many victims of sexual abuse coming forward in 2017–2018 with the support of the #MeToo movement, it is hoped that no story will be forgotten, because the stories need to be told. However, it is very difficult to tell these stories, no matter how many others may come forward. While many who are coming forward were abused by trusted doctors, clergy, teachers, supervisors, and others in power, children who suffered sexual abuse by a parent or family member are less likely to come forward because

- they have no other group support,
- they are told no one will believe them,
- they are threatened with harm by the abuser, or
- they are not sure how to tell the rest of the family what is happening to them.

Even when stories are told and children do speak up and ask to be heard, the fact is that the courts are at odds with the people when it comes to the definition of justice. There is great disparity in what we expect and what we actually get from the courts.

It is important to identify and support the best interests of the child, but when this is a crime of adults against children, it is difficult to provide justice to the children because it is more important to keep the children safe. Therefore, most judges make decisions for that moment in time. Decisions are not made in the best interest of the child for the lifetime of the child. Instead, judges determine the best interest of the child to keep them safe from the abuser *at that moment in time.* In most instances, settlements are made through mediation to keep the children safe, but that results in the story being silenced. The child is safe, but the abuser usually agrees to this type of settlement only if the case is not made public and the victim (child) agrees to never revisit this abuse within the legal system. This robs the victims of the healing potential that comes from true justice when the truth comes out in public and the abuser is held accountable.

CHAPTER 2

Educating Parents and Providing Resources

When I was a little girl, I never imagined growing up and marrying a pedophile who would abuse our children. I never imagined the challenges of working through a legal system where the offender has more rights than the abused.

The man who committed such a crime is one of many who were never held accountable, who were not prosecuted, and who did not go to jail because the children were so young. And he is someone's neighbor, someone's uncle, now someone else's daddy, and no one knows he is a pedophile who will continue to abuse children, as he knows from experience that he can get away with it with no consequences.

What Is Child Sexual Abuse?

Sexual abuse is inappropriately exposing or subjecting a child to sexual conduct, activity, or behavior. A parent, or anyone, who exposes a child to any type of sexual behavior or pornographic material is abusing that child. This abuse is a crime and is referred to as incest when it is among family members.

Ninety percent of childhood sexual abuse victims are abused by family members and trusted adults. Statistics show that 88 percent of sexual predators are male (RAINN

2018). People who sexually abuse children have power over that child, and their actions cause the child to feel powerless.

As mentioned earlier, one in every seven girls and one in every twenty-five boys will be sexually abused before their eighteenth birthday. Every year, more than four hundred thousand children are victims of childhood sexual abuse. This is the conservative number, based only on reported cases. Because most children do not report, the actual number of victims is much higher (Rainn.org 2018 and d2l.org 2018).

In the United States, there are an estimated sixty million survivors of sexual abuse, of which forty million survivors are under the age of thirteen (Merryn 2004, 2012).

Survivors are everywhere.

What Are the Signs of Child Abuse?

Most victims do not show any physical evidence of their abuse unless the child is very young and the parent is still helping them with toileting and bathing. And even then, it may not be apparent unless the child says something. However, there are a few things to notice that may cause concern such as any genital irritation, infection, or painful bowel movements. More often, behavioral signs are most common. One of the first behavioral signs in younger children is regression in a child's development, where they act younger than they are, such as returning to wetting their bed or sucking their thumb. Any of the following may be cause for concern and certainly reason to talk with a physician:

- behavioral regression
- depression
- anxiety
- anger
- change in personality
- change in behavior
- changes in artwork—how and what they draw
- loss of appetite
- withdrawal from normal activities
- substance abuse
- self-mutilation
- acting out sexually
- fear of certain places or people
- bed-wetting

- night sweats
- nightmares
- thoughts of suicide
- mental health issues

It is important to note that childhood sexual abuse victims are three times more likely to be at risk for mental health conditions as nonvictims. Mental health costs related to childhood sexual abuse were estimated at $20 billion per year in 2007–2008 (Rohde et al. 2008; Waldrop et al. 2007). In 2018, according to the Children Safety Network Economic and Insurance Resource Center (2018), these costs increased significantly. Childhood sexual abuse costs for United States victims include overall costs to the health care system:

- Sexual abuse against children, ages zero to fourteen, costs $71 billion every year.
- Sexual abuse against adolescents and young adults, ages fifteen to twenty-four, costs $45 billion per year.

Talk to Your Child

It is important that all parents talk with their children to make sure children know the dangers of sexual abuse. If any parent ever has a concern, they should talk to their child.

What do I do if my child says they were sexually abused?

Believe them!

- In 96 to 98 percent of child abuse cases reported to officials, children's statements were found to be true (NSW Child Protection Council, 1998; U.S. Department of Health and Human Services, 2013, 2014), which means less than 2 to 4 percent lie about this crime.
- However, only one in three adults indicated they would believe a child if they disclosed sexual abuse (Australian Childhood Foundation 2010; RAINN, 2018).
- Seventy-three percent of child victims do not tell anyone about the abuse for at least one year (Broman-Fulks et al. 2007).
- Forty-five percent do not tell anyone for five years. (Broman-Fulks et al. 2007).
- Only about 38 percent of child victims disclose the fact that they have been sexually abused (www.d2l.org 2018).
- Some never tell anyone of the abuse (www.d2l.org 2018).

How Do We Help?

Most importantly, believe a child who comes forward to tell about sexual abuse, and offer support. Children who have been abused often feel like it was their fault. They feel shame and feel like there is something wrong with them. They should be told it was not their fault, they did nothing wrong, and they did not deserve what happened to them. The stigma they perceive is based on how they feel about what happened to them. It is important to try to reduce this feeling of shame and help them to no longer feel this stigma so they can try to move forward with a positive self-image.

They judge themselves and think others will judge them, and it is critical to help them understand that no one will judge them; instead, they will support them, because no child should ever have to experience such a heinous crime.

Helping the child move from feeling like a victim to feeling like a survivor is one of the most important actions a parent can take. The child needs to be reminded that they have survived the most difficult experiences of their lives. The child needs to be told they are powerful to move forward, showing their strength and bravery by telling someone what happened and accepting the support offered by family, friends, and helpful professionals.

How do we remove the perceived stigma attached to childhood sexual abuse for all victims?

We can only do that by becoming more comfortable in speaking about sexual abuse. When adults have difficulty discussing this topic, children pick up on the undertones, and that is why they feel others are judging. The truth is very few people are comfortable talking about sexual abuse because it is such a heinous crime. Now that people are learning more about the actual statistics and numbers of survivors of childhood sexual abuse, there is a demand for action. Parents and communities are coming together to fight for the rights of their children.

Society at large needs to embrace these children and support them. People need to understand that these are tortured souls who lost their innocence and are suffering in ways no one else can imagine unless they too have experienced this type of abuse. Life is very difficult for survivors who feel there is a stigma attached to something they had no control over. They need to know it is okay to talk about this and to ask for support when needed, without any concerns of how people will react. They need the strength to stand up, demand to be heard, and demand that the abuser face the consequences of this heinous act.

As one sexual abuse survivor of the May 2018 case against the Archdiocese in Minnesota stated "Even when you're kneeling, even when you're stumbling, you've got the legs to stand up and hear your voice…Speak your truth, because what happens is you make change… and you make the world safer." (New York Times, May 31, 2018)

The #MeToo movement has provided an opportunity for the perceived stigma to be diminished by all of the people coming forward to show the magnitude of the problem, but the victims still feel it exists because of how they feel about what happened to them. Hopefully, the #MeToo movement will continue to document how many people have survived sexual abuse and, as a result, help to remove the perceived stigma associated with it.

How do you help children understand it was not their fault and they are going to be okay because they are strong and brave in coming forward?

Sharing books written for children on this topic can be very helpful. One especially powerful book is written by a child who was sexually abused; she wrote the book to help other children. The book is *Please Tell! A Child's Story about Sexual Abuse*. The little girl, Jessie, was eleven years old when she wrote and illustrated this book.

Another very helpful book for children is *No More Secrets for Me* by Oralee Wachter. It is a book for adults to share with children.

One more book that may be helpful is *Do You Have a Secret?* by Jennifer Moore-Mallinos. This book talks about good secrets and bad secrets and helps children realize that all secrets are not fun and okay. It helps them to know what to do if they feel like they have a bad secret instead of a good secret.

All of these books can be ordered from Amazon (www. amazon.com). I would recommend that every community public library and every school library have these books available for children.

What do you say when someone tells you they or their child was sexually abused?

Most people do not know how to respond because they are shocked or surprised or uncomfortable. If someone trusts you enough to share this very personal and vulnerable information, look them in the eye with kindness and say,

"I am so sorry this happened to you." Then hug them, and it is okay if tears stream down your face as you hold them and let them know it is okay if they want to talk about it.

What Parents Need to Know

While there are many organizations working to address the overall concerns of childhood sexual abuse, locating this information can be overwhelming to parents who have just discovered their child was abused.

- **How to report this abuse**. Reach out to your local authorities or to your pediatrician, then to an attorney and a child psychologist who specializes in child sexual abuse.
- **How to find a therapist or psychologist.** To find a professional for the child to document the abuse, ask local authorities, attorneys, or your child's pediatrician. You can also use the internet to search for local therapists with sexual abuse as a specialization.
- **How to deal with Child Protective Services**. Tell the truth about everything you know. They are trying to help protect your child. Child Protective Services is responsible for investigating child abuse that occurs with parents and others legally responsible for a child. Their primary concern is the safety of the child. It is important for the parent to know that when dealing with the child protective services, when they interview your child, you will not

be in the room – the child alone is interviewed. They will interview the parent individually and the child individually – not together. This is to make sure the child is safe and not influenced by any parent.

- **How to deal with the local authorities**. Tell the truth about everything you know. You want to make sure your child is protected from the abuser. Ask for a restraining order while you are documenting the child's story of abuse. When dealing with the criminal justice system, the parent and the child will be interviewed separately – not together. The child is the center of every interaction and it is to protect the child to interview them without any parent in the room.

- **How to remove the child from the abuser**. Immediately ask for a restraining order. You can get this with the help of an attorney or by going directly to the local authorities. Most people think that those who sexually abuse children are arrested after the police report but that is not the case. Very seldom are sexual abusers arrested. They can only be held for up to 72 hours without specific charges based on evidence and even if they are charged with a crime, most are released on bail or on personal recognizance. Generally, most people think these cases will go to trial. Again, that is not the case and most often a plea deal or mediation will be settled for child sexual abuse cases. And even when a case does go to trial, it can take a year or more to get through the system. Therefore it is critical to obtain a restraining order against the abuser to keep the child safe throughout the process.

- **Who is responsible for the costs?** If the state moves forward with criminal charges against the abuser, the state incurs the costs. If they tell you it is in the best interest of the children to move forward with a civil case, the nonoffending parent bears the costs. If social services deems this to be a credible case, the county will cover the costs of child psychologists and therapists even if the case moves forward as a civil case. If the case is a civil case and mediated in the best interest of the child, the nonoffending parent pays the attorney and mediation fees.

Where Do Parents Find the Resources to Help?

There are many organizations that provide helpful information available by telephone and websites. If you do not have a computer at home, go to your local public library. Below is information on how to access immediate resources by telephone or by using the internet.

- RAINN (Rape, Abuse & Incest National Network) is the nation's largest anti-sexual-violence organization. RAINN created and operates the National Sexual Assault Hotline. That phone number is 1-800-656-4673 (1-800-656-HOPE). This hotline is in partnership with more than a thousand local sexual assault service providers across the country. RAINN also supports programs to prevent sexual violence, to help survivors, and to ensure that perpetrators are brought to justice. Their website is www.rainn.org. The following can be found on (and is copied from) their website.

Child Abuse / Sexual Abuse:

- National Child Abuse Hotline: They can provide local referrals for services. A centralized call center provides the caller with the option of talking to a counselor. They are also connected to a language line that can provide service in over 140 languages. Hotline: 800.4.A.CHILD (1-800-422-2253)
- Darkness to Light: They provide crisis intervention and referral services to children or people affected by sexual abuse of children. Hotline calls are automatically routed to a local center. Helpline: 866.FOR.LIGHT (1-866-367-5444)
- Cyber Tipline: This Tipline is operated by the National Center for Missing and Exploited Children. Can be used to communicate information to the authorities about child pornography or child sex trafficking. Hotline: 800.THE.LOST (1-800-843-5678)
- National Children's Alliance: This organization represents the national network of Child Advocacy Centers (CAC). CACs are a multidisciplinary team of law enforcement, mental and physical health practitioners who investigate instances of

child physical and sexual abuse. Their website explains the process and has a directory according to geographic location.

- Stop It Now: Provides information to victims and parents/relatives/friends of child sexual abuse. The site also has resources for offender treatment as well as information on recognizing the signs of child sexual abuse. Hotline: 888-PREVENT (1-888-773-8368)
- Justice for Children: Provides a full range of advocacy services for abused and neglected children.
- National Sexual Violence Resource Center (www.nsvrc.org) has published a very helpful document: "The Advocate's Guide: Working with Parents of Children Who Have Been Sexually Assaulted" (Yamamota 2015): www.nsvrc.org/publications/nsvrc-publications-guides/advocates-working-parents-children-who-have-been-sexually-assaulted.

Guidance for Nonoffending Parents

I never imagined having children who would be sexually abused and working with child protective teams, social services, and law enforcement.

Nonoffending parents have many questions when they are heartbroken over what has happened to their children. It is difficult to think clearly. Do not hesitate to ask for help and guidance. You cannot possibly know what you need to do to protect your children in situations like this. Make sure you have a solid and credible psychologist/therapist for your child; they can help direct you with everything else. You, as the nonoffending parent, will also benefit from individual therapy as well as group therapy with other nonoffending parents of children who were sexually abused.

How does anyone cope with this revelation? What signs were missed? What can you do to keep yourself and your children safe?

- Take one step at a time, and do ask for help and guidance.
- The most important thing to remember is believe your child and show them how much you love them.
- Remind them it was not their fault.
- Follow the steps and work with local authorities to ensure the safety of your child through any needed restraining orders.

How do you forgive yourself as the nonoffending parent for not knowing earlier what was going on?

- First, concentrate on what you need to do now that you do know.
- You must be a survivor to protect your children so they can be survivors.
- You will always wonder how this could have happened. Your heart will be forever broken because

of this heinous act committed by a loved one to your child.

- But you will take charge, and you will protect them, and you will never miss any future signs.

How do you find the right therapist/psychologist for your child?

Finding the right therapist or psychologist is critical. You need to find someone you and your children are comfortable talking to and feel you can trust.

Your children's physician or the Child Protective Team, Social Services should be able to appoint a psychologist with a lot of experience in this area. The psychologist should document everything for the children. This is especially important because the mind can help repress the memories of what happened. But the psychologist also knows the child will remember at some time in the future, so they need to document everything for when the child does remember.

Repressed memories are memories that have been unconsciously blocked because the memory is associated with a high level of stress or trauma. Although someone may not recall a memory, it may still be affecting them subconsciously. Sometimes these memories emerge later into the person's consciousness.

Below are some examples of how a therapist might document what your child shares when they talk about what happened to them.

(From the therapist/psychologist)

Dear Child,

My name is Dr. B, and I am the counselor you came to see after you got very brave and told your mommy about your touching troubles with your daddy. You were only four years old, and it was so scary to talk about "the games" Daddy played. We began working on this scrapbook so you could remember exactly what happened to you. You are very brave, and you are very kind. You have done a good job in counseling, and you understand you have done nothing wrong. You had lots of courage to share your secret, and lots of people believed you.

(From law enforcement)

Dear Child,

I understand you started a scrapbook, and I wanted to be part of it, so I am writing you a little note to let you know how brave you were when you told me what was happening with your daddy. You were very brave coming into my big detective office and talking about "grown-up" stuff. I see a lot of children like you, and I know how scary it can be to talk about some of the things we talked about, and especially when we are talking about a person we love and look up to. I just wanted you to know how proud I was of you. You were very much believed, and I apologize for not being able to do more than we could. But when you get older, you will study and understand more about the criminal and judicial system and how it works (or in this case, does not work). Remember you are very courageous and brave for sharing your secret and telling the truth.

The Impact of Childhood Sexual Abuse on the Child

Children who have been sexually abused are more likely to have learning issues, to disassociate, and to have addictions, eating disorders, anger issues, panic attacks, and many other health and behavior problems.

What does it mean when the therapist says, "The child may disassociate in the future"? It is important to understand that anyone who has experienced childhood sexual abuse may use disassociation as a coping mechanism.

Disassociation is a coping skill used to separate the person from the traumatic event, as well as from memories of a traumatic event. People who learned to disassociate as children when they were being sexually abused often disassociate at any time in their lives when they are in a traumatic or unsafe situation. This means they are able to mentally remove themselves from the physical situation they are experiencing. This is how they protect themselves. The problem is some children who were sexually abused will find themselves victims of more abuse in the future because they developed the ability to disassociate as a child during the sexual abuse. If something happens to trigger a memory or make them feel unsafe, they may subconsciously begin to disassociate and therefore not realize what is happening to them until it is over. And that means they may experience more pain and suffering at the hands of other people who may take advantage of them.

What does this mean for parents? You should ask for more information about anything you don't clearly understand.

- **What might trigger a change in my child's behavior?**
  A trigger could be anything about any situation that causes a reaction in a child.

- **What is a coping skill?**
  These are skills needed to manage emotions that come at unexpected times for unexpected reasons – coping skills are needed so when something triggers a memory or reaction in a child, they know how to manage their reaction.

- **Will my child be in danger if they disassociate?**
  Yes, they will be in danger.

- **How can I prevent my child from further abuse?**
  Talk to your child and help them identify strategies to stay safe.

- **Is there a way to prevent my child from the possibility of addictions?**

Talk to your child and with their therapist. Make sure you ask the therapist to help your child understand how to use appropriate coping skills.

- **What signs do I look for?**
  Any changes in behavior, appearance, anything that suggests something is not quite right or quite the same as you would expect from your child.

- **What can I do?**
  Learn everything you can and ask the psychologist/therapist for guidance. Pay attention to the details of your child and how they behave and how they feel. Do not live in denial. As mentioned earlier, there may be no signs; your child may appear to be handling things well, so keep communication open. Be sure to have at least one day a week where you spend one-on-one time with your child.

Clinical psychologists and therapists work with the victim and, as appropriate, with the family. Communication is very important. Insist the therapist explain to you what the child may experience in the future and what signs you should look for to keep them away from harm. Ask them to write it down if your children are very young, so you do not forget as they grow up and become teenagers and young adults.

Everyone in the family has been impacted. Even if the abuser is removed from the home, the nonoffending parent is overwhelmed with grief and heartache for what has happened to their child.

Ask questions. This is a topic none of us are prepared to understand. There are no stupid questions; they are all important. After all, your child's future life experiences are at stake.

What should you do? Ask for help. Who do you ask? First, ask the therapist who worked with your children. They are most concerned about your child's best interest. They can direct you to resources. Local authorities should be able to direct you to resources as well. If you have a computer and search the internet for advice, and many people do today, make sure you are working with a reputable site. There are many reputable organizations with helpful information, as mentioned earlier in this chapter. Try to work with local organizations that can support you. Let them know specifically what your needs and concerns are, and if you are not sure, tell them you don't know and ask them, "What do I need to know that I have not asked about?"

Because it cannot be said enough: what should you do when a child tells you they have been sexually abused?

BELIEVE

Believe them! Kids do not make up this kind of descriptive information. Someone has to expose them to this before they have knowledge to talk about it and tell someone.

- Believe them.
- Get them out of the situation.
- Support them.
- Ask what you can do to help them.
- Let them know you will keep them safe.
- Ask for the name of a respected psychologist and a criminal/family attorney who can help all of you through this time.

The Impact of Sexual Abuse on Children as They Are Growing Up

It is important to emphasize that early childhood sexual abuse has serious long-term traumatic consequences for the child. When a child is sexually abused by a parent (or trusted adult), the physical, emotional, and psychological damage is overwhelming and lasts a lifetime. Even when they move to a new environment and try to make changes so everything doesn't remind them of the past, it is somehow still in the back of their mind. And every time someone asks, "Why don't you have a dad?" they really don't want to tell them the truth about what he did, as most people will not understand. So take some time to talk with your child about how to handle questions about their family. Today, there are many different types of families, so explain to your child that not everyone has a mother and father at home. Many children are raised by only one parent, and some are raised by grandparents or other relatives. If you live in a conservative, traditional town or your child goes to a conservative school, many of those children may have more traditional family situations, so someone may ask about your child's. Talk to your child about what they would like to say. You must be very careful so they do not feel they have a reason to be ashamed or feel bad because they no longer have a father. Most of the other kids really are not concerned; it is more likely that their parents want to know the situation. Let your child know it is fine to just say, "I live with my mom." Then you, as the parent, can share information as appropriate with the other parents. It is important to remember that most people are not comfortable with the topic of childhood sexual abuse, so keep information simple and just say, "We are divorced, and the father is no longer in the picture."

Child sexual abuse impacts children differently at different ages and stages of life. The abuse can take on different meanings and have additional impacts as the child goes from a preschooler to a teenager to a young adult as they understand the abuse and what happened to them in slightly different ways as they grow up.

As a young child, knowing you were sexually abused is a terrible thing. If they were abused by a parent they trusted, it is especially devastating. Even if the child understands and knows that it was not their fault and they did nothing wrong, it still hurts. The pain is still there. The child feels cheated out of their childhood. The innocence of childhood is lost, and they now have trust issues, as it is hard to trust anyone when they were hurt by a family member who was supposed to protect them and keep them safe.

As they get older, the understanding of sexual abuse and what happened to them can be the root of many problems.

As they reach puberty and attend sex education classes in school, what happened to them may trigger unexpected feelings and confusion. If the child remembers the details, the child may realize just how truly terrible it was. They won't understand how a trusted parent could have done that to them, and they now have to figure out how to have a healthy teenage experience. They have issues they can't explain and don't understand.

Disassociation and Blackouts

Because the brain does try to protect us from traumatic events and as a result often represses these memories, the child may not remember the early abuse and may not realize they have issues until something triggers that memory. It may happen when they go on a date and someone kisses them or touches them or does something that causes them to have a flashback of something—sometimes a memory, sometimes a bad feeling, but something affects how they are able to deal with growing up and dating.

As mentioned earlier, disassociation is a coping skill used to separate the person from the traumatic event as well as from memories of a traumatic event. Some children actually black out or disassociate and have no memory of what happened. They are at great risk of danger if they do black out or disassociate, as they are not aware of what is happening to them. Others may have panic attacks and feel intense fear or discomfort that comes on immediately and may not last very long but could include sudden pounding of the heart, sweating, or shortness of breath. Others may begin to tremble or shake or feel like they cannot breathe.

The child may not know why they feel the way they do, so be sure to talk with a professional who can help them understand their feelings. Children who have been abused are especially confused about sexual issues and sometimes make decisions for the wrong reasons, or they totally black out or disassociate and therefore are not aware of what is happening to them until it is over. Be sure to talk with a mental health professional who understands your situation; they may be able to help you and your child develop strategies and coping skills during this difficult stage.

Trusting and making good friends is difficult. Going on their first date is stressful—wondering what to do, what is okay, will they be a friend, will they freak out if someone kisses or touches them. You worry that your child won't have a normal teenage response. You worry they will freeze and overreact or disassociate, so you don't know if you should let them go out with their friends. It is important to emphasize that children may react in a variety of ways, and the parent will need to figure out how to help them through everything based on that individual child. The solution could be different for each child. This is why it is especially important to have your child working with a therapist to develop coping skills for your child's specific needs.

The transition from childhood to adulthood should be the most exciting times of a child's life, but it is scary for teens who were sexually abused as children. They don't trust others, and they may not trust themselves to act appropriately. They may not even be sure what is appropriate. So find someone for you and your adolescent child to talk to who makes your teen feel more confident and safe.

Sadness and Anger

Feeling sad is normal, but pay attention to the signs. Sometimes abused children get so sad they become depressed. They may withdraw into a place where you as a parent can't reach them. Then when they are ready to talk they look very troubled. They may remember bits and pieces, or have confusing or bad feelings and not know why. They may feel abandoned, and every time they see a movie where a father is reunited with a child, deep down they may wish they had a safe father to reunite with, not a pedophile/ sex abuser father who will harm them.

Feeling anger and expressing anger more and more as they get older is not unusual. It may get worse when they reach puberty. As abused children go through puberty, changes in their bodies may remind them of bad images of things that happened to them when they were little. They may get mad, but they may not want to talk about it, and they may not remember the details of what happened or why they feel this way; something just triggered the reaction.

Life is hard enough for teenagers, but it is extremely difficult and filled with many more challenges for children who were sexually abused.

Child Abuse, Addictions, and Suicide

Children who were sexually abused are more likely to experience various addictions, including alcohol, drugs, eating disorders, and compulsive actions. According to specialists in the addiction field, an estimated 90 percent of their patients have a known history of some type of abuse (Blume 1990; ; U.S. Department of Health and Human Services, 2013, 2014; Finkelhor et al. 2014). Substance abuse, including alcohol, drugs, and food, is a common consequence of early sexual abuse. Many survivors also have abusive relationships and problems with intimacy. Further, a majority of children and adolescents who attempt suicide have a history of sexual abuse. Survivors of childhood sexual abuse are ten to thirteen times more likely to attempt suicide (Plunkett et al. 2001; Finkelhor et al. 2014).

Addictions and obsessive-compulsive behavior are especially common among incest survivors. Addiction is common because chemical use/abuse/addiction serves a survival purpose, as it numbs the pain and creates a sense of feeling alive or excited for someone who may feel "dead" inside. This dead feeling is one many survivors have because of childhood sexual abuse. Eating disorders are also an addictive behavior; the survivor is so preoccupied with food and weight that they focus on little else. Obsessive-compulsive behaviors are irrational or excessive behaviors that provide temporary relief of some inner struggle while they are engaged in this behavior, which may include things like compulsive shopping, eating, gambling, even exercise (Blume 1990; Leeb et al. 2011; Finkelhor et al. 2014).

These are all serious concerns and real consequences of childhood sexual abuse. This is why it is critical to make sure these survivors of childhood sexual abuse have access to a psychologist/therapist who specializes in childhood sexual abuse and can help them develop healthy and appropriate coping skills.

Many children/teenagers do not want to participate in treatment for sexual abuse, and boys are particularly reluctant to talk about or admit any history of sexual abuse.

If there is no treatment, many of these survivors do not see any connection with later experiences of addictions, ongoing abusive relationships, feelings of self-loathing, inability to trust, or problems with intimacy.

Living with the Knowledge That Your Child Was Sexually Abused

As a parent, you are devastated and heartbroken that your child was sexually abused. You feel responsible that you were unable to prevent this from happening. You never forget, and you never forgive yourself. Even if you didn't know what was going on until you were told by your child, you always feel that you should have known earlier and that you should have been able to prevent it from ever happening. You no longer trust anyone to be alone with your child. You feel like you have to be constantly overprotective and suspicious of anyone who comes in contact with your child.

The fear you experience—the panic attacks ... waking

up with nightmares … he is trying to hurt your children again—never goes away. You overreact to protect your children. You go overboard to make sure they are happy. You try to give them whatever they ask for because you know they have lost so much, but that is not always a good reaction or decision.

You try to slowly build a network of trusted friends and family so your children feel like they have many people looking out for them, but it is difficult. Make sure you, as the parent, continue with any needed therapy, as it is often difficult to know how to rebuild trust and how to make the best decisions for your children. Talking with a professional can be very helpful, as you may need to develop appropriate coping skills and seek guidance on how to best parent your child so they become a strong survivor.

3

Surviving Childhood Sexual Abuse

Some children tell their secrets of abuse, but many do not. For those children who do not tell, they have a very difficult time and struggle throughout their lives, not understanding the full impact the abuse may have on their ability to have healthy relationships. Further, they keep this secret inside, not realizing how wrong it was for the abuser to harm them in this way. They internalize their feelings, and even if they forget, they are not aware and therefore do not get the support needed to help them move forward and regain a positive self-image. Moreover, they continue to feel powerless to the abuser and others who try to abuse them in the future.

For those who do tell but do not get support, life and the legal system do not seem fair. Many children tell their parents or loved ones and are not believed. Or they may be told not to tell anyone else, and then they feel ashamed and stigmatized. Further, they feel those they shared their secret with must not care about them because the abuser's heinous crime is not acknowledged and they continue to feel powerless to the abuser.

When a child does not tell, or when no one believes or supports them and there is no treatment, many of these survivors do not see any connection with later experiences of addictions, ongoing abusive relationships, feelings of self-loathing, inability to trust, or problems with intimacy.

What would you say to a child who was not believed or who did not get help for a long time?

Tell someone and keep telling until someone believes you. And even if many years have passed and you did not get the help you needed, it is extremely important to tell someone. It is critical to get the mental health support you need so you know why you have experienced life in the way you have, and to have someone acknowledge that a terrible thing happened to you as a child, you did not deserve it, and it was not your fault.

What would you say to the child who does tell and who does get support?

Even when children do tell and are believed, and even when they receive needed support, they still experience the long-term impact of childhood sexual abuse with many of the lifelong struggles mentioned earlier. The difference is, these children have the support of family and friends, and they hopefully have guidance from a mental health professional/ therapist who can help them develop the needed coping skills.

Note: The remainder of this chapter is written to help the parent understand how the child might feel after telling their secret, so it is written as if directed to the abused child, not the parent.

You Told Your Secret, and Now You Are Safe

When you were little, you were sexually abused. You told someone what was happening, and now you are safe and removed from the abuser. The abuser had power over you then, but you were strong, and you took that power away from the abuser by speaking up and telling what happened to you. Life is better now. Sometimes you remember, and it hurts, but for the most part, you are doing okay. It took a lot of courage to talk about what happened to you, and you know you are brave, but sometimes you feel confused. And sometimes you feel angry, and sometimes you feel sad, but at least you feel safe, and that is a good thing.

You feel safe and you feel good because you told someone, and they believed you, and they removed you from harm. You may even feel powerful because you told and you were believed, even though the person who hurt you told you not to tell anyone. They told you no one would believe you or they would think it was your fault. Well, you told anyway, and everyone believed you: your mom believed you, the doctor believed you, the sheriff and the detective believed you, Child Protective Services and the psychologist all believed you. You were very brave to share your secret, and now the abuser is far away from you and unable to hurt you anymore. So you feel strong and brave, and you know it was not your fault, and you know people believe you and will keep you safe. And that is a good feeling.

For a while, you feel so relieved that is all that matters, and you begin to relax and enjoy life. But as time goes by and you get older, even though you go about what appears to others as a perfectly normal life, you never forget that something bad happened to you. It is very difficult to get over something like this when you feel cheated of your childhood and your innocence. Your scars are invisible to others, but you know they are there. Life is not fair—you feel this way often, and it is okay to feel this way.

Abusive Parent and Termination of Rights

If you were abused by a parent, the impact is far greater, as you lost your innocence and trust to someone you loved and trusted. You suffer the actions of a heinous crime, you lose a parent, and if that parent remains a threat, their legal rights are terminated.

If the abuser will not abide by restraining orders and continues to try to see the child despite the restraining orders, the judge may decide it is in the best interest of the child to terminate that parent's parental rights in order to keep the child safe. This means that, by law, that parent now has no legal relationship to the child. Legally, that parent is no longer the child's parent. While most abusers welcome this termination of rights because it means they are no longer responsible for the child, financially or in any other way, the nonabusive parent now bears sole responsibility for the child, financially and otherwise. The nonabusive parent is now solely legally responsible for the well-being of that child.

Grandparents

You also may lose grandparents and family members who choose to believe the offending parent (abuser), as no one wants to believe their child would sexually abuse their grandchild. The choice has to be made to support the victimized child or the abuser. When the support is not for the child, the child loses even more family and feels deeper rejection and greater loss.

The nonoffending grandparents are concerned. They love the children, but they may not realize these children now need extra hugs, extra one-on-one time, and a lot of support. They may not understand why their teenage grandchild has a difficult time in the dating world. So they push and make comments, not realizing the abused child has to deal with growing up and dating in their own time, in their own way, due to their early childhood abuse.

The parents of the offending parent will likely not want to believe their child would abuse their grandchild in this heinous way, so they do not believe the grandchild. The children who are removed from the offending parent may also be removed from these related grandparents for safety reasons. This is more often the case when the parental rights of the abuser are terminated.

Strategies for Sharing Information with Family Members

Most family members do not want to believe any child would be sexually abused, and they certainly do not want to think it could happen to someone in their family. No one wants to believe their child, or a niece or nephew, or grandchild was sexually abused. Most people are not comfortable with this topic and do not want to believe it could have happened to someone they know and love. Many act like it never happened, and they don't understand the needs of these children. It is easier for these family members to live in denial than to deal with the realities of how to support the victimized child.

What can parents say to help relatives understand what has happened to the child? Difficult as it may be, it is important to tell the relatives this really did happen. The children did not lie about this, and devastated as everyone is, they need to accept the truth and put the child first in order to support the child. It is important to tell relatives the following:

- Do not question the child about the abuse. If the child wants to talk about it, let the child raise the topic.
- Do not tell the child you heard about it and do or do not believe them. Children do not need to worry that everyone is talking about them because of this abuse.
- Do not start to treat them differently than you did before.
- Follow their lead. If the child trusts you enough and wants to talk about it, believe them and just listen and hug them and tell them you are so sorry this happened to them, that it was not their fault and they did not deserve for this to happen. Also tell

them they can come to you any time and you will keep them safe.

- Do continue to treat the child like you always have—teasing them and laughing and letting them know how much you love them.

Guidance for the Abused Child Whose Family Has Been Made Aware

- Remember that no matter what anyone may say, you have told the truth, and you were very brave. You are believed, and you are now safe.
- If someone says something that makes you uncomfortable, just say you do not want to talk about it.
- If you need help or you feel confused or scared, tell someone so they can help you.

Guidance for a Child Who Was Not Believed

Keep telling someone what happened to you until someone believes you!

Guidance for Those Who Did Not Get Help

It is never too late to get help. Tell someone and let them know you need and want help and support.

A Special Note to the Teenage Survivor

(To be shared by a parent or by the family psychologist/therapist.)

Try to understand how much pain your nonabusive parent must have felt when you told them what happened to you— and how much pain they still feel. Try to understand how much they need you to love them and trust them, as they were also very strong. And when you can, thank your parent for all they did to remove you from harm. Many nonoffending parents don't know how to get their children out of unsafe settings, but if your mom did, you can believe it was not easy. Your mom believed *you*—not the person who was her husband and your biological father. She believed you. She protected you even when others may have said, "How can you be sure? They are just children. How do you know they are telling the truth?" Your mother believed you because she knew you could not have talked about those things if they had not happened. Your mother believed you and protected you, so when you can, try to understand what that really meant for her. She had to go to court, and she had to face the abuser. She had to explain to family and friends why his parental rights were terminated, and if she found that didn't work, she probably moved you to another setting. She had to find a way to support the family financially by herself, and she had to keep you safe from the abuser, who continued to violate the restraining order. She has done her best by you, so appreciate what she has done. Don't blame her for not knowing. Thank her for acting and protecting you as soon as she did know. What she did took a lot of courage, just like it took a lot of courage for you to tell what happened to you. You have a brave mom, and you are very brave. You are both survivors.

4

A Parent's Life after Their Child Shares Their Secret

Parenting the Abused Child

After the child shares their secret and the child is removed from the abuser, the nonabusive parent tries to help the child move forward and have a healthy and happy life. While the child is still young and recovering, they appreciate the fact that you believed them and removed them from the abuser. As the child gets older and involved in school life, they make friends, they tuck this far away in the back of their mind, and they try to forget what happened to them. You see changes in their personality. They are often happy and less withdrawn. They are still cautious, but you can tell they are relieved and feel safe.

Then, as they become teenagers, parenting may become more difficult. When the child thinks about what happened to them, it can take on a whole new meaning. It is even worse for some to remember or think about what happened to them because they are now at an age where kids talk about sex. The memory of what happened to them is renewed in a different way and in an even more horrible light. They may act out because they now don't understand how you (the nonabusive parent) could have let that happen to them.

They are no longer the victim you saved or removed from harm, but, for some—not for all, but for some—you are the person who didn't protect them and prevent the abuse from ever happening. You didn't protect the survivor from the abuser. This can be a very difficult time. Although you removed the child from the abuser as soon as you found out, as they become teenagers, some may think you should have prevented it from ever happening. As teenagers who begin to think about their own future, boyfriends, girlfriends, getting married, and having children, what you didn't protect them from is something they just cannot understand. They are still grateful you removed them from the situation, but they may begin to wonder why you couldn't keep it from ever happening at all. They may tell you they would never let anything like that happen to their child. Part of this behavior is due to being a teenager, and their teenage years are even more complicated by the impact of childhood sexual abuse.

Nonoffending parents relive their guilt every day. It doesn't matter that you did not know. It doesn't matter that you did everything you could to protect them as soon as you did know. It doesn't matter that your own dreams were crushed and that you will always have a broken heart because of what happened to them, that you have moved away from everything you know to keep them safe. All that matters to some of them now is thinking about how stupid you must have been not to know what was going on and prevent it from ever happening. Many teenagers think their parents don't know anything, but your kids know you didn't know anything about what happened to them, and that was why you could not protect them from the very beginning. You couldn't possibly have good advice for them now. This specific situation varies from child to child and family to family. But if you find this is how your child is acting, then a good family counselor may be critical to surviving and keeping your family and yourself healthy. Just as the abused child knows that life isn't fair, you, too, know that life has not been fair to you. You did not dream of growing up and marrying a pedophile who would abuse your children. And although people say to get on with your life and get over this, they do not have a clue. You are lucky to be out of the situation, and you are grateful you were able to remove the children from continued abuse. But it is still very hard sometimes.

Strategies for the Parent

Love your kids regardless of how they act. Try to determine why they may be acting a certain way so you can provide any additional support they may need. Remind them they have already experienced the worst thing that can happen to them and they have survived it well. Treat them like survivors who can move forward with happy and productive lives. Do not treat them like victims who cannot overcome what has happened to them. Children who become victims of child abuse can still experience a full life. Let them know you believe in them.

Victims/survivors behave in different ways, and some have more challenges than others. Be prepared to try to understand them, and do not take everything they say to heart, as they will grow out of this teenage stage and once again remember how you were very brave and strong when you removed them from their abuser.

For the nonoffending parent, life is very hard. You believe your child, and you do what is right by your child. You are horrified that the man you married, the father of your children, or a family member or a friend or neighbor, or clergy member or teacher could possibly abuse them in that way. If it was your husband and the father of your child, you find yourself a single parent, and if he does not go to jail and if his rights are terminated in the child's best interest, you find yourself with no child support and only your income. You may still be in fear, not knowing where he is or when he will break the restraining order again.

Although you don't want to think about it every day and you want to get on with your life and theirs, life is hard as a parent of a sexually abused child. It is especially hard for a single parent of a child who was sexually abused. It is even harder when all children in the household were abused. You are resentful, you are angry, you are hurt, and life is not fair for you either. It is okay to feel that life is not fair. But also take time to acknowledge the fact that as soon as you found out, you did stop the abuse. You believed your child, and the abuser was removed from the home and from the family. You were also very brave and a survivor. You love your children and are grateful they are so amazing, so strong, so brave, and so resilient.

As your children get older, you worry about leaving them alone, and you worry about what they will think about. You worry about what they think is okay and not okay. You worry about what they will remember. Even though someone made them do those heinous acts, it is still a terrible and frightening memory, and you are not sure how they will deal with it. Again, it takes on a whole new meaning when they are teenagers. You may need to find a good psychologist with expertise in childhood sexual abuse to help you and your family work through these memories.

It is important to help your children look at themselves as "that child" in their memory; it is not who they are now. It was not who they were then; it was what someone else made them do and that someone was a family member or other adult whom they trusted when they were too small to stop it and keep it from happening. If the child psychologist assigned to work with your child by Child Protective Services does their job right, they will document everything in a special book for your child, and they will take a handprint of the child at that time so that later in life the child can see how small they were when they spoke up and shared their secret.

Scenario/Reflection: Something's Not Right Inside

Child: "I don't know what's wrong. Everything is okay at school, and with my friends, but it's like something isn't right inside me. I have been to lots of doctors, and they can't find anything wrong. Why do I feel this way?"

Parent: "I don't know. I recall the first time my daughter just went into a kind of zombie state. She wouldn't eat much, watched a lot of TV, slept a lot, and was very moody.

Dr. Jekyll and Mr. Hyde became her nickname. I thought it was just that she was having a tough time, as this all began when she was twelve and got worse when she was thirteen. I thought she was sick, so I took her to a lot of doctors. One day, I was so concerned I was telling a friend who knew that she had been abused as a young child, and he said, 'Maybe you should find someone for her to talk to … she may be remembering.' I had really hoped she would not remember what happened to her as a young child. But if she was going to remember, I wanted her to have a professional to help her through those memories."

If your child is acting depressed or distressed, find out why. Get professional help for yourself and your child. There are psychologists who specialize in childhood sexual abuse. Make sure you find out all you can about those you think may be appropriate for your family. It is very important to choose someone you and your child are comfortable with, so schedule an initial consult to see if this therapist is right for the needs of your family.

A teenage girl who had been abused as a young child had a very positive experience when her mother took her to a therapist specializing in teenage girls who had been sexually abused as a young child. When the girl came out of her first session, she said, "She really understood me. She really knows how I feel. I feel so much better now that I talked with her. Do you know this happens to a lot of other kids? Not just me. She works with lots of girls who had similar experiences. She understands me and says it is okay to feel the way I do."

This sense of validation is extremely important. No

matter how much a family member may try to understand and help the abused child, the visits to experienced psychologists can provide a sense of relief and hope that are crucial to the now teenage girl, so she moves from having been a child victim to a child survivor to hopefully a thriving adult who is not defined by what happened to her as a young child.

On the other hand, a teenage boy who had been abused for several years as a very young child had a less successful experience with the therapist. Even though the therapist came highly recommended, it turned out to be a bad choice. When the boy went in, the therapist was very uncomfortable and said, "Do you know why you are here?" This immediately caused the boy to become uncomfortable. The boy had become disinterested in school and angry, with no explanation, causing the mom to become concerned. This particular therapist did not begin the first session getting to know the child but instead set up a hostile environment in which the boy would not open up and talk. To make matters worse, the therapist immediately said, "The first thing we need to do is have the boy take some tests to make sure he does not have any of the pedophile tendencies that his biological father (the abuser) had." This was totally inappropriate considering the purpose of this visit. It made the child feel worse about everything, because no one had ever expressed concern to him that he might have the pedophile problem as a result of his own abuse. The boy became very scared.

It is important to clarify that, as a parent, you do not need to worry about an abused child growing up to be like their pedophile father. Children are 50 percent of both parents; they are not 100 percent of an abusive parent. Further, statistics show this is only a concern when the child is not removed from the abuse throughout their entire childhood and teenage years, and therefore, this is all they know. When a child is removed from an abusive situation, the child will be out of that environment and will understand this is not acceptable behavior. Moreover, as that child grows up and remembers what was done to them and the relief they felt when removed, the child is far more likely to protect other children than to abuse them.

Needless to say, there was no return visit to this therapist, and the family began to try to find someone else who truly was experienced and ready and able to deal with the issues the child was having. Unfortunately, the boy was no longer interested, as that experience made him distrust therapy. So he would not try any other therapist until he turned twenty-eight years old—more than fourteen years after his terrible experience with the wrong therapist.

It is important to note that sexual abuse is a difficult topic because most psychologists do not have continued in-depth experience with survivors who come forward and share their secrets as a young child but then need to come back to talk with someone during their teenage years. Rather, they have experiences with children who come in and talk about what happened to them. They see them through initial counseling, as required by the court or as needed by the child and family. They have less experience with children who shared their secret as a young child, have been removed from the abuser, have been living a pretty normal life since that time, with repressed memories of their child abuse, and who are now teenagers with a different set of issues, all related to the sexual abuse they experienced when they were so young (even though the child may not realize these issues relate back to those repressed experiences/memories).

Some of the psychologists said they were not certain what their role should be when the issue has already been confirmed; they were trained to help confirm whether a child has been abused, to help the child at that time, or to help adults much later in life as they begin to remember what happened to them as children. They had less experience knowing what their role would be and how to be helpful when a child came to them as a teenager. If the child has moved, the child may not be returning to the same therapist who treated them initially. Today, with rising statistics and with more victim/survivors coming forward, academic institutions are training psychologists/ therapists to be specialized in the lifelong consequences of childhood sexual abuse, to provide positive support and coping skills during all stages of a survivor's life.

Anger and Confusion during the Teenage Years

It is important to realize that everything is not always about the childhood abuse. All teenagers have difficulty growing up and knowing who they are and what they want to do. With the peer pressure and the stress of school, many children who have not been abused have anger and feel depressed. So, do not assume that every problem the child has is related to the abuse. This can be difficult for the nonoffending parent, who may relive and remember the abuse more often and in a different way than the abused child.

Repressed Memories

As the nonoffending parent, you will remember everything your child told you about what happened to them. Because the brain has a way to repress these memories over time to protect the child from the continued stressful memories and pain, you may remember things that they do not remember as the years go by. Later, they may begin to have flashbacks or disassociate as different experiences trigger those memories of childhood sexual abuse.

Ask questions and listen to your child. Always ask, "Why do you think you are feeling this way?" And if they say it has to do with school or friends, it probably has to do with school or friends. If they cannot explain why they are feeling this way, and you are concerned, then try to find a good psychologist who has the appropriate expertise. If your child is a teenager, find someone who specializes not only in childhood sexual abuse but also in teenager issues.

CHAPTER 5

Healing from Abuse

Child survivors of sexual abuse are often overlooked in the healing process until after they become adults and have failed relationships and dysfunctional lives. This is because they may not tell anyone of their abuse until they are adults. And for those survivors, life is especially challenging, as they do not have the additional support to help them understand why they may be struggling with life.

Most survivors of childhood sexual abuse experience PTSD and need to be treated. Post-traumatic stress disorder is a mental condition that results in a series of emotional and (or) physical reactions in individuals who have experienced a traumatic event. PTSD includes a variety of physical conditions, such as headaches or migraines, dizziness, fatigue, chest pain, breathing difficulties, and stomach and digestive issues. It is also common for those with PTSD to suffer nightmares or flashbacks of what happened to them. These symptoms can be very scary for the child because they are reliving their trauma all over again. They can also experience depression and anxiety, and they may lose interest in activities and friends. It may affect their ability to sleep at night or even focus on a single task.

Survivors may experience PTSD as well as personality

disorders, different types of anxiety issues, abandonment issues, learning disabilities, low self-esteem, eating disorders, inappropriate sexual behavior, drug and alcohol abuse, and many more issues. For the child survivors who do tell, they can begin to heal from the moment they are heard, believed, and supported.

As the healing process begins and continues, it is important that all professionals working with these children and adults treat them like survivors—not like victims.

- The child needs to know they have survived, and they can still have a healthy and happy life.
- The child needs to learn appropriate coping skills for the challenges they will face throughout life.
- The child needs to feel empowered for having come forward with the details of their abuse.

If you are a survivor and need to talk to someone at any time during your life, don't put it off. Talking to someone can help the healing process. You will always be healing, but you can be a successful, loving, wonderful person because you have already survived the most difficult time of your life. So everything is looking good, and you are happy, but there may be times when you are overcome with a feeling or a memory, or just overwhelmed with life but not sure why. It is important to deal with it *at that time*, with a professional therapist.

Remember—although this terrible act happened to you, you now have the power and control, and you are moving on with your life.

Make sure you work with a therapist who is trained in childhood sexual abuse, as it is very helpful to have validation of what happened to you and understanding of the challenges you face.

Should You Press Criminal Charges?

If you told someone about your abuse and they believed you and removed you from the abuser, but the abuser did not go to jail, then you may be wondering if you should press criminal or civil charges when you reach age eighteen. At age eighteen, you are legally considered an adult, and you can press charges on your own. Prior to age eighteen, you are still a minor, and the nonoffending parent has to press the charges on your behalf.

But what do you expect to get from this action? Many abused children hope the offending parent will apologize and say how much they regret what they did. However, most pedophiles/sex abusers do not believe what they did was wrong, and most will not admit their guilt. Most victims/survivors are disappointed with the outcomes of criminal cases and civil cases. Again, it is important to think about what you hope to gain from this action. Whether it is a civil or criminal case, the abuser has to be found guilty, even though the burden of proof may be less for a civil case than for a criminal case. A civil case involves private disputes between persons, while criminal cases involve an action that is considered to be harmful to society as a whole. Child sexual abuse is harmful to society at large, but sometimes the judge determines there is not enough evidence for a criminal case and therefore suggests the family utilize the civil courts.

The emotional pain is the same for the victim/survivor for both types of actions, civil and criminal. You have to decide if it is really worth dealing with all of these feelings, knowing that you may or may not win the case. If the abuser did not go to jail at the time of the crime and his parental rights were terminated *in the best interest of the child,* it could be that this is the best that can be done—a decision that was made that removed the abuser from the child to keep the child safe but did not send the abuser to prison for his actions, which were very wrong, and which were indeed a heinous crime.

Should You Face Your Abuser and Ask Them to Take Responsibility for Their Actions?

Some abused children hope the abuser will ask for or be required to participate in an apology session. However, this too is usually a disappointment because it requires the abuser to admit guilt. Much has been written about the pros and cons of adult children who were abused facing their abuser (Davis, 2008). The pros (advantages) are that you have the opportunity to face your abuser and tell them how their abuse has impacted your life. You can tell them how you trusted them, and they violated that trust, and it has caused you irreparable harm. The cons (disadvantages) are that more often than not, the abuser has no remorse, no guilt, and therefore will not admit what they did or express any remorse for how it has impacted your life. This could cause you even more pain. The bottom line is, are you willing to do this even if you do not get the admission or an apology? Will you feel better or worse when this is over?

Neither pressing charges nor facing your abuser should be done without previous counseling and a good therapist by your side who will help you through your feelings as you go through this process.

Some lawyers will say, "We don't need a therapist to prove you have suffered. I can do that." Remember the purpose of the therapist in this instance is not to prove your suffering but rather to help you emotionally and psychologically as you relive your abuse when facing the abuser in any civil or criminal action. The therapist may also be helpful in documenting various mental/medical health issues resulting from the abuse.

The most important thing to remember is you have used your power, you have told your secret, and you were believed and removed from the abuse. Although this terrible act happened to you, you realize you now have control and are moving on with your life. You may find it helpful to write a letter to the abuser—even if it is not used in court and you never send it. Writing down how you feel may help you feel better.

The following are examples of these types of letters.

To the abuser from the abused child:

> You didn't want to be a daddy enough to be good. I remember what you did to me. I trusted you, and you hurt me and made me do bad things. How could

you do that? How many others have your hurt? I wish you went to jail. Mom would have taken you to criminal court, but the judge said we were safer this way. But when I turn eighteen, I can make that decision myself. You better be ready to answer my questions.

To the abuser/offender from the nonoffending parent:

I am writing this letter to document how our lives were affected by your abuse. When you sexually abused our children, it was unforgiveable. They trusted you, and you betrayed that trust. When they told me what you did to them, I knew they were telling the truth. The signs were there; I just had not wanted to see them. But when both children provided such detail and described specific acts, I knew it was true.

When you refused to admit what you did and the only way to keep them safe was to have a restraining order, which you violated, and then when you terminated your parental rights because you didn't want to go to the counseling the judge mandated, and you provided no child support, they truly felt totally abandoned. As my son said, "You just did not want to be a daddy enough to be good." You didn't love them enough to stop playing the games and go to counseling. You would rather give them away—walk away and never see them again—if you couldn't continue to sexually abuse them. That is very hard for any child to understand. As a family, as well as individually, we all feel we were cheated out of a lot of things.

As a wife, I feel cheated of my childhood dreams. No one dreams of growing up and marrying a pedophile—having that person abuse their children and then terminate their parental rights so they don't have to pay child support—and being left to raise two children who were sexually abused by a trusted parent. I am devastated. My childhood dreams did not come true. I did not marry my knight in shining armor. I do not have anyone to share my dreams with. I have nightmares and always worry about the safety of my children. Your threats to kill us all if we took you to court are the only thing that kept you out of prison. But it also made me appear weak to the children, and you have had a wonderful life getting away with the most heinous of crimes. I only wish that you regretted your actions, but I know you do not have the capability to feel regret or remorse, and you cannot be helped because you refuse help. So we have to live in fear of how you will break the restraining order next time, and what will happen when they decide to confront you when they are old enough. I will never forgive you for what you did to them, to me, and to our family.

You had a son and a daughter who loved you once. You betrayed their love and trust, and I have had to help them understand that no matter what you may have done to them, they are still the most amazing kids in the world. I work hard every day to try to keep them with a strong self-image. It is hard for any child who was sexually abused by their father, then abandoned when that father terminated his rights instead of doing the right thing, which would have been to get the court ordered pedophile/sex offender mental health therapy and to want to pay child support to make sure they were okay. But you really did only want them for your selfish, inappropriate, and truly heinous acts.

My heart will never heal, because every time I look at them, I remember what you did to them as very small, trusting children. I worry about their first sexual experience of their choice, and I have no way to prepare them for what they may or may not remember—if they will have flashbacks. What memories will it bring out for them? You have no right to life and happiness, so it is a cruel joke that you have your own life with no responsibilities for your actions and no conscience to keep you awake at night.

CHAPTER 6

Case Studies Related to Decisions Made in the Best Interest of the Child

Decisions are made every day by parents, lawmakers, teachers, priests, judges, and community and political entities regarding "the best interest of the child." Although there is no standard definition of "the best interest of the child," the term generally refers to decisions that courts make when deciding what type of services, actions, and orders will best serve a child, as well as who is best suited to take care of a child. Most of these decisions result from a need to make a decision in the best interest of the child at one point in time, based on a specific situation.

The information provided here comes from a legal case and follows the survivors for over twenty years, focusing on the impact of the abuse as well as the decisions related to "the best interest of the child," when the children were victims of sexual abuse from a family member—specifically in this case, the father. This case is important because 34 percent of people who sexually abuse a child are family members, and 88 percent of people who sexually abuse children are male. Although this case study addresses childhood sexual abuse by a family member, specifically the father, it is important to note that the impact of the abuse on the children, are the same as the impact of any sexual abuse on any child by any person. The child survivor may suffer even more when it is a parent, but all children who have been sexually abused have many challenges throughout life as a result of this abuse.

What the courts did and did not do is all too indicative of our legal system's inequities and experts' and decision makers' lack of knowledge about their roles and responsibilities when it comes to ensuring the safety and, indeed, the best interests of the children they serve.

These stories have to be told so they are never forgotten. They are about children who did tell and who were believed, but justice was not served, and in fact, some were actually silenced as a result of mediation and settlements.

The information provided here represents only a few of the many stories of victim/survivors who should know they are important and they deserve to tell their story so that no one forgets about the many children who suffer this heinous crime. These children should not be forgotten. Nor should their offenders be forgotten and ignored as they may remain free to continue victimizing more children. The stories must be told, and the legal system must take responsibility for protecting the rights of children, not only for that moment in time but also during the lifelong consequences of childhood sexual abuse.

Many of the issues identified here are considered common issues relating to the impact of childhood sexual abuse, which means there are many studies that document these same effects of childhood sexual abuse on most victims. This book provides further documentation to show that many of these victims do survive and spend a lifetime coping instead of living life to its fullest.

The information provided here covers different critical issues over a twenty-five-year period, beginning with the first few years of the child abuse and spanning the next twenty years of growing up and dealing with the impact of that abuse on these children. Specific issues have been identified to help families of survivors be better informed of the continuing long-term consequences of child sexual abuse.

The information is provided from different perspectives at different points in time to show the continuance of issues and to document specific critical points for informational purposes.

The names used in this legal case have been changed to protect the privacy of the individuals and families.

Case Study—Setting the Stage

"Why does Daddy make us play that game?" Sister asked Brother.

As Mom listened in, she was shocked to hear about the game so she stepped into the room and asked, "What game is this?"

Brother said, "It's a special game Daddy plays with us. It's a secret, so we can't tell."

Mom was worried, so she sat down and said, "It's really okay to tell me."

Both children said, "Daddy said no. We will be in trouble if we tell you or anyone. It's his special time with us."

Sister and Brother were almost three and five when Mother overheard the conversation. She said, "We never keep secrets in our family, so you can tell me."

Brother said, "Daddy taught me when I was 2. Then Daddy taught Sister. When I asked Daddy why Mommy never played the game with us, he said when we got really, really good at this game, then we could tell Mommy and ask her to play."

Mother was devastated, and as the tears started rolling down her face, she knew what they were telling her had to be true, as children that young could not make up that kind of detailed information. She called the pediatrician and an attorney. They referred her to a child psychologist, who talked at length with the children. When they came out, the psychologist said she had contacted Child Protective Services, who would then bring in the authorities. The children were interviewed first by Child Protective Services and then by the sheriff and a special detective.

The children were young but very credible. All professionals who interacted with them believed the children, but the logistics and realities of taking these young children through the often harsh and very adult legal system was not deemed to be in their best interest.

Although the sheriff's office, the psychologist, and Child Protective Services all believed the father had sexually abused these two children, his constant efforts to break the restraining order and threaten the family caused the courts to say, "We can only protect the children by terminating the father's parental rights but not by criminal court and jail time, because even if he went to jail, he would get out in a few years on good behavior, and the family would be at even greater risk for his continued threats."

Restraining orders were put into place, but the father continued to break the restraining orders. No one felt safe, so the mother and children were constantly on the move. Moreover, both of the children suffered PTSD from this abuse, as well as learning disabilities, addictions, disassociation, blackouts, abandonment issues, anger and trust issues, and many other health and behavior problems.

The mother, the nonoffending parent, went to therapy for nonoffending parents. The son went to therapy and made a book with important letters from everyone who interviewed him, documenting what happened, including letters from the sheriff's office explaining the problem with the legal system and why it did not work in this case. The daughter had no therapy, as she was determined to be too young, although she was able to show the therapist with dolls what Daddy did to her.

The mother was now a single parent to two sexually abused children, and she had to get a job to support the family, as the offending pedophile father did not have to pay child support when his rights were terminated. It was the father who, after being told he had to complete the court-ordered pedophile sex offender therapy in order to ever regain supervised visitation with the children, stated, "I will not pay child support for children I do not get to see, and I refuse to complete the pedophile sex offender therapy even though I signed an agreement to do so as part of the settlement. But I will terminate my parental rights, and I will pay no child support." So the judge considered the many times the father broke the restraining order, the fear the children were experiencing, and all the legal documentation proving the abuse and determined it was in the best interest of the children to terminate the father's parental rights. So the mother tried to move forward with the responsibility of two children even though that meant she had to relocate away from her family to get work to support her children.

The psychologist who was counseling the abused children during this time was excellent. When the counseling was completed, she suggested the mother treat the children like normal kids and not focus on the abuse and try to move forward with life. She did not explain to the mother that these children would not only suffer a lifetime of PTSD but, during their adolescent and young adult years, may disassociate; have nightmares; remember what happened; be hospitalized for various reasons, experience alcohol and drug abuse, as well as addiction and eating disorders; and be victimized many more times by others because of disassociation and blackouts—all a result of the childhood sexual abuse by the father.

No one prepared the mother or the children for what the future held. The lifetime impact of the abuse resulted in daily struggles and many mental health issues for both children, while their father who criminally sexually abused them for over four years never experienced any jail time, paid no child support, and was allowed to move on with his life, with no public record to protect other children from his pedophile sex offender behavior. He was living life with no remorse or consequences.

Was there justice for the children? The family wondered many times if justice had really been served, knowing the abuser had terminated his parental rights, paid no child support, served no jail time, and had no public record as a sex offender. Which of the following might explain the decisions that were made?

- Was it because the abuser was an officer in the military with ties to high-level officials in Washington, DC?
- Could it be that our legal system provides tools for the perpetrator to continue their abusive behavior rather than providing justice for the victim?
- Could it be that it really was in the best interest of the children because no one was willing to risk the threats and behavior of this man, and the courts were just trying to do the best they could to protect the children, given the laws at that time?

It could be that the termination of the abuser's parental rights at the time of the crime was in the best interest of the children at that time, to keep them safe, even if the abuser did not go to jail for that heinous crime—and that was the best that could be done for the safety and well-being of the children.

This happened in the early 1990s when incest and childhood sexual abuse were not talked about. Today, over twenty years later, even though we know so much more, we still do so little to protect our children and to provide needed treatment and support to the victims and survivors of childhood sexual abuse.

How wrong is this? How dysfunctional and unjust is our legal system?

Survivors of childhood sexual abuse struggle every day just to function. They learn to cope in whatever way they can. After all, the life they are living is the result of decisions made in the best interest of the child.

These decisions need to take into consideration:

- what is in the best interest of the child at this moment in time
- what additional assistance needs to be provided throughout the child's life to ensure they have the support they need for any mental health issues resulting from this abuse
- the need for the family to understand the many challenges they will have as they go through life.

Families need to know how to protect the abused children from more abuse due to disassociation and other related PTSD issues.

Decisions need to be made in the best interest of the child *for life*.

Questions That Should Have Been Asked

It is important to understand the case study that inspired this book.

This most heinous of crimes committed by the father has resulted in a lifetime of coping and trying to survive for both children. The nonabusive mother has dealt with guilt since that time, as no mother can understand how she could marry a man who would sexually abuse his own children. No one dreams of growing up and marrying a pedophile who abuses their children and living with the lifelong nightmares that go with that heinous act.

The Early Years

This is the story of a family. The wife, Kathy, was a professional with a PhD, having earned her doctorate at a major research institution. She married an officer in the military who was a graduate of the Naval Academy. They were both in their thirties when they met and married in Washington, DC.

A year later, their first child was born, a son named Matthew, and two years later, a daughter named Mary. The abuse began when the son was about two years old, while they were living in the Washington, DC, area. The abuse of the daughter began sometime after her first birthday, when they were living in England.

As with many families, from the outside everything seemed to be fine. They were professional parents who seemed kind and caring. The children were seen laughing and playing. There were no obvious signs that would cause concern.

When the mother, Kathy, came home from the hospital with the new baby, a little girl named Mary, she found her son, Matthew, who had just turned two years old, crying and running from Daddy to cling to his mommy. He did not want her out of his sight.

At the time, all of this seemed somewhat acceptable. A

new mother came home; the two-year-old wanted to cling to Mommy, who had brought home a new baby. But in retrospect, those were actually telling signs of trouble to come. As it turned out, this may have been the first time the father sexually abused the two-year-old son, while his wife, the mother, was in the hospital with the new baby.

Within a week to ten days of Kathy coming home from the hospital with the baby, Matthew started running a very high fever. They took him to the pediatrician and were shocked to find that he had a staph infection of his genital area. The doctor simply said, "You must do a better job of keeping him clean." William immediately blamed Kathy, and she was stunned that Matthew could possibly have a staph infection, as she was always extra careful with cleanliness and the children. The pediatrician never suspected sexual abuse because the parents were professionals and because William was a charming officer who knew how to say the right things at the right time. In retrospect, this was clearly a missed sign. Matthew had to stay at the doctor's and be given penicillin by injection because the staph infection was so bad.

What should the physician have done? Were there other questions he should have asked the family? Questions for the child or the parents?

The physician should have asked the family specific questions regarding why they thought the child might have a genital staph infection. Further, the physician should have asked Matthew to talk with him without the parents in the room. The physician should have asked Matthew if anyone had touched him or played any games with him that involved his genital area.

Another telling sign was that the son never wanted to be left alone with the father and never wanted to go anywhere alone with him. Again, the father always explained this by saying, "This is normal. He is jealous of his new baby sister and wants to stay with his mommy."

Just before Mary was one year old, William got orders for Europe, and they were transferred to England to head up some highly classified international partnerships. Kathy took this as a good opportunity to take a leave from work and be a full-time mother to her young children.

They found a lovely home with a traditional English garden and a gardener and were very excited about their new adventure. Mary and Matthew would have their first and third birthdays in England. What looked like a wonderful family adventure was about to turn into a family nightmare that would last a lifetime.

As the family settled in, William traveled daily by train to work in London, while Kathy and the kids settled into their new home. Kathy and William became acquainted with their neighbors, and the children began to have play dates and go to the parks. They made day trips to see the sites, went on picnics, and spent family time together.

One day, Mary came running to Mommy and complained that Dada had hurt her. Kathy took Mary to the doctor, an American doctor at the military base, and the doctor just said, "You know kids say all kinds of things. Don't worry about it." But Kathy did worry about it, and as the winter wore on, Mary was always sick with a sore throat and usually strep throat, and Matthew would go to sleep every night before William came home from work. Matthew said he didn't want to stay up and see his daddy. Matthew became very depressed, and the doctors referred him to a psychologist at age three. William expressed great concern and took off work to take Matthew to the psychologist, and as a result, Matthew did not talk about anything.

What should have happened? The doctor should have asked more questions to determine if Mary and Matthew were in fact in danger and if they were being hurt in any way. The psychologist should have talked with Matthew without his father in the room to find out what might be causing the depression. Instead both doctors deferred to the officer status of the father and did not consider the concerns of the child.

Kathy began to worry about her children. She knew something wasn't right but couldn't put her finger on the problem.

One night when William came home from work, he took Mary to the bathroom with him. Kathy went to see what was going on, and William slammed the door and told her to go away. Kathy then knew for certain she had to go back to the doctor. This time, she told the doctor of her specific concerns, and he said, "Look, your husband is an officer with a lot of connections in Washington. You should leave this alone. I'm sure it's nothing to worry about."

Kathy then asked to see another doctor, a female doctor, who upon examining the children said, "I understand your concerns, and it is true that Mary has strep throat and pneumonia again, and Matthew is still very depressed, so I can recommend you take both children back to a warm climate to see if they can get well and stay healthy." So Kathy went home and told William the doctor thought Mary was having too many cases of strep and pneumonia. She was only two, and Matthew had been seeing all kinds of doctors, including psychologists, because of his lethargic behavior. Kathy told William the doctor suggested she take the children and visit her family in Florida. William wasn't sure it was a good idea but finally agreed, since the doctor recommended it and he didn't have much choice.

When Kathy got to Florida with the kids, she spent her time trying to see if the warm weather and time with family would help the children get better. The kids played, went to the beach, and enjoyed time with cousins and grandparents. Kathy wondered if perhaps she had overreacted.

As the Christmas holidays approached, Kathy told the children that Daddy would be coming for Christmas. Matthew said, "No, Daddy is *bad*. I don't want him to come."

And Kathy said, "I know Daddy sounds angry sometimes, but he isn't bad." _What should Kathy have asked Matthew?_ Kathy should have asked Matthew, "Why do you think Daddy is bad?" But she didn't.

So, William came, and once again, the children became despondent while he was there. When he left to go back to England, the children said they were glad Daddy was gone.

Kathy thought it was just because they hadn't seen him in a couple of months. But when William came to visit again in March, Kathy knew something was very wrong.

She woke up one morning and went downstairs. There she found William and both children naked, running around. When she asked what was going on, William said, "Oh, I was getting a shower, and the kids decided to take off their clothes and run around the house." The children had never done this before, so Kathy was confused. And then William picked Mary up and said, "She's still my little girl," and Mary blushed in a way Kathy had never seen before.

When William returned to England, the children, who were now three and five, said they were glad he was gone. When Kathy went into the kids' room later that week, Mary was talking to Matthew about a game Daddy played with them—rocket ship to the moon. Matthew said it was a bad game, and when Kathy asked why, Matthew told her he didn't like the game. When Kathy asked how they played it and Matthew told her, she cried, "No, no, Daddy wouldn't play that kind of game with you."

But Matthew said, "Yes, Mommy, he does." And as the tears streamed down Kathy's face, she was devastated because she knew her children could not provide the details unless they had experienced what they were telling her.

Kathy didn't know what to do, so she looked up the name of an attorney and placed a call to the attorney and the pediatrician.

Kathy also put in a call to the Navy Family Help Center, and they said, "William is a high-ranking officer. Previous domestic violence and abuse cases have not ended well when handled by the military. We suggest you get an attorney and file a civil case. Your husband has too many contacts in Washington. We really cannot help you, as we cannot protect you." Kathy was shocked. The military could not protect her and her children from the father who was abusing them; the military was telling her to go through the civil court system, which meant she would have to find the money to do that. She had hoped the military would support her and her children, as her husband was an officer, but instead they were very clear; they could not help her because of previous failures of the military to protect families against abusive officers.

Kathy called the pediatrician, who recommended a psychologist who specialized in child abuse, someone who could talk with the children and call in the child protective team, social services, and the law, if indeed the allegations were true. The psychologist interviewed the children and then referred the case to the child protective team, social services, and family court. Matthew had to give his statement to the sheriff and a special detective. Then the navy detectives got involved because it became a family court case and William was in the navy.

Kathy had to be interviewed by the child protective team and social services. Matthew had to be interviewed by the child protective team, social services, the county sheriff, a special detective, and a naval investigator. Matthew was five years old and considered old enough to interview. Mary was only three, and although she could show with dolls what her daddy had done to her, she was considered too young to interview. Kathy was cleared as not knowing what William was doing to the children and labeled the nonoffending parent by Child Protective Services. William remained under investigation and was required to receive treatment from a psychologist whose specialization was working with pedophiles and sex offenders.

Child Protective Services and the child psychologist decided it was in the best interest of the children for Kathy to file for divorce and ask for sole custody of the children, and get a restraining order so William could have no contact with the children. This would be the best way to protect the children from the offending father. When William returned to Florida, he was met at the airport and handed a court-ordered restraining order stating he could not go near his wife or children. William retired from the military at age forty-three, having served twenty years with the navy, to start a new career as a financial adviser in Florida.

Although the restraining order stated he could not live in the same town as Kathy and the children or come anywhere near them at any time, he violated the restraining order numerous times—at the beach, in their home, where they went for gymnastics, even at school and church. The key to protecting children with a restraining order is to make sure the leaders or organizers where the children are have a copy of the restraining order; that is the only way to enforce the restraining order. Kathy made sure everyone had a copy of the restraining order. When William would show up, he was told he had to leave, and then the preacher or the principal would let the family know he had come into the school or church to see the children but had been sent away. However, each time law enforcement was notified, they did not arrest William for violating the restraining order but instead told him not to do it again. So the children continued to be afraid because they realized he would continue to break the restraining order since he faced no consequences.

The divorce was dangerous for Kathy and the children. William violated the restraining order not only with them but also by leaving his business cards on the front doors of the personal homes of the judge and some of the psychologists and therapists who were witnesses, as well as the preacher at the church where William violated the restraining order. He was trying to intimidate the witnesses, and he succeeded.

Unbelievable as it may seem, there was nothing the courts could to. The judge had to recuse himself because the same laws that gave William so much freedom did not give judges any leeway. Because William had left his card on the judge's front door at the judge's home, it could be seen as an intimidating tactic, so the judge had to recuse himself because of perceived conflict of interest, as the judge could now have a personal fear of William that could interfere with his objectivity in the case. As a result, all of the witnesses became nervous about their involvement with the case. The judge said that although it was clear what William's intent was, he was still in the gray area of the law and could not be arrested for any crime. Kathy was finding that in the state of Florida, the victims had far fewer rights than the offender.

After all legal work was completed, William got off with restraining orders in place, and he terminated his parental rights. Even though this meant that Kathy and the children would receive no child support or any income from William, the courts found that this was in the best interest of the children since they did not believe the children should have to face their father in court at their young ages of three and five, and that the trauma of seeing their father who had abused them would not be in their best interest.

Matthew continued with therapy and made a book about his life with his daddy. It was a very sad but powerful book, and it had pictures that he drew of what William would do to Matthew and Mary. The book was powerful because it showed the brave little boy who spoke up to share his secret and tell about the sexual abuse by his daddy.

It also included letters from his psychologist confirming and documenting that she believed this brave little boy, and letters from the sheriff and special detective, stating they believed the little boy and apologizing for the failure of the legal system to protect the child. She explained how the legal system should work but in this case didn't work. This was very powerful documentation of the sexual abuse suffered by these children.

After the court issues were settled, Kathy had trouble finding a job that paid enough to support herself and her children in the small town where her family lived in Florida. William had decided to buy a home and settle down working as a financial adviser within one hour of where Kathy and the children were living, so Kathy decided to look for work back in the Northeast, where she would have a better income and connections with friends from graduate school and not have to look over her shoulder every day for William, who continued to violate the restraining order.

Kathy had not seen any signs when she first met William. He was educated and charming, a true officer and gentleman. When she became pregnant, he had apples and cheese waiting for her when she came home from work. He had her sit down and put her feet up, and sometimes he would make her chocolate-chip cookies. He was thoughtful and appeared to be caring, and he really wanted children. There was nothing to indicate he was a pedophile who would abuse their children.

No one told Kathy what impact the abuse would have on her children throughout their lifetime. She wanted desperately to pretend none of this had happened. She wanted her children to have a "normal" childhood. What she didn't understand was that this would never be; they had lost their innocence and trust to their biological father, and they would have difficulty developing healthy attitudes about trust and relationships.

Kathy threw herself into her work, trying to pretend that if she did, she would not have to think about what happened to her children. She had been told by Matthew's therapist that the best thing she could do was to raise the children without focusing on the abuse and give them as normal a childhood as possible. So it wasn't that Kathy didn't pay attention; she just did not realize what additional issues the children would have throughout the various stages of their lives.

Mary had a lot of problems with inappropriate friendships with boys. And Matthew still had too many memories and wished he could have protected his sister. He worried that he had not been a good big brother, although he was so very small and young when it happened. He was angry at what his father had done to both of them, and he still feared the threats of what his father would do to him if he ever found him.

Although the courts had changed the last names of the children so they no longer carried their father's name, the children now carried their mother's maiden name to maintain the important sense of family. By not changing their names to something totally different, however, the children remained targets of the offending biological father whose rights had been terminated. He knew how to search for them and continually broke the restraining order with no legal consequences.

Kathy was not told the following:

- Her children would suffer from depression during puberty and disassociation with events that triggered their childhood trauma.
- Her children would be easy victims to others, even their own age, for inappropriate behavior—as well as easy victims of older teenagers who took advantage of them.
- Her children could black out or disassociate and not be aware of what was happening to them in social or other settings.
- What was "normal" for children who had not been abused was not "normal" for them, as they responded differently or would black out or disassociate or feel strange in some way.
- Addiction is common for incest survivors.
- Obsessive-compulsive behavior is common for incest survivors.
- Eating disorders are common for incest survivors.

What Should Have Happened

William should have gone to jail and served time. The reason given why he didn't: the courts said the family would be safer if he did not go to prison. Based on previous experience, they believed the family was safer with William terminating his parental rights, paying no child support and having no rights to the children. They said the children would be in continued danger if he went to prison and then was released after a few years on good behavior.

The criminal courts believed it would be too traumatic for the children to testify against their father in court and believed it would be in the best interest of the children for the father to terminate his parental rights.

A plan should have been put into place to support the wife and the children, who were all victims impacted for life by the heinous crimes of the father. Even though the wife, Kathy, was a professional, this was unfamiliar territory; she knew nothing about child abuse and even less about childhood sexual abuse. As the nonoffending parent and the wife of a pedophile/sex abuser, she too was a victim. She needed therapy for her own PTSD issues. Kathy did not get the continued therapy she needed, and the children did not have continued therapy, because it was determined they should get on with being kids and try to live as normal a life as possible.

Teenage Years

When Mary was fourteen, she had several traumatic experiences. The first led her to the ER, where she was treated for everything except psychological and mental health concerns. She was in great pain, hysterical and panicked, but no one knew it was because she had been unknowingly raped. She disassociated and blacked out when her sixteen-year-old male friend started to touch her and ended up raping her. She did not know what had happened until it was over and she "woke up." But she did not tell anyone because she felt ashamed and stupid. She did not know, as no one had warned her or her mother that this could happen to her. They did not know that she should not be left alone with anyone who might take advantage of her, because she could black out or disassociate.

Mary found that whenever she was in an uncomfortable situation, she would disassociate and therefore not know how to stop what was happening to her until it was over and she became consciously aware that something bad had happened. After another similar incident, she tried to commit suicide, because she was sure she just could not take any more of this. When she went home and told Kathy what happened and how she tried to throw herself in front of a bus, but someone pulled her back just in time, Kathy got on the phone with Dr. B, the psychologist who had treated the children when they were younger. She asked what she should do. Dr. B said she would recommend a therapist for Mary to see. So Kathy dropped everything at work and got on a plane with Mary to take her to see an expert therapist back in Florida who had access to the children's previous records.

The financial aspects of meeting her daughter's mental health needs continued to grow. Kathy had a good job, but every time she had to take Mary to another doctor and take time off from work, she was told, "You better be careful taking off so much time if you want to keep your job." Even when the employer knew her children had mental health issues, they were not supportive and threatened her with a choice of her children or her job. On the one hand, society says, "We understand. We have moved forward, and you can talk about these unconscionable acts," but on the other hand, there are no safety nets in place to support the mother (also a victim of these circumstances) who needs to attend to the mental health issues of her children and also needs to keep her job, as there is no child support to help with expenses.

As all of this was going on, William violated the restraining order yet again, by trying to contact the children via the internet. They discovered it when Matthew had a school assignment to search his name in Google to see what information came up. Matthew was shocked to see a statement: "Your biological father is looking for you." This was a very scary find, and everyone in the family panicked. Once again, Kathy had to get an attorney to follow up regarding yet another problem with William violating the restraining order.

The children were teenagers, ages fourteen and sixteen, when they had to go back to court, as William continued to break the restraining order by trying to track them down on the internet. Once again, there was no justice, as the judge said, "We cannot know for certain it was William and not someone else using his computer who did this." The children continued to live in fear while the man who criminally sexually abused them got off again. The judge suggested they go to mediation to work things out. That means each party gets an attorney, and they go to a mediation attorney the judge suggests, and each party tells their side of the story. Clearly this was not in the best interest of the child—to work things out through mediation with a man who had sexually abused his children, terminated his rights, paid no child support, and continued to break the restraining order. Clearly the judge was not held accountable for protecting the children and making decisions in the best interest of the children. Where was the justice for the children who had already suffered so much?

So the family went to mediation with the abuser, provided the documentation once again, and threatened criminal proceedings if he would not stop violating the restraining order. This resulted in an agreement where William was to obtain an irrevocable life insurance policy with the children named as beneficiaries upon his death, but the children and nonoffending parent had to agree to drop all charges of child sexual abuse going forward, which meant there would still be no documentation of this pedophile and his abuse. This resulted in the silencing of the victims in order to get some form of future financial support for their continuing mental health needs. So the victims were silenced by the mediation agreement, and there was no justice served in condemning the abuser, as the case had to remain closed even though the children would receive no financial support for many years until the time the life insurance policy was paid upon William's death.

This mediation experience was quite traumatic and resulted in more PTSD for both children. Matthew had a lot of anger issues during his teenage years, but he did not talk about why he was feeling the way he was or what he was going through that caused him to be so angry. Boys often do not acknowledge the impact of childhood sexual abuse, and with repressed memories, he wasn't sure why he was so angry or why he had difficulty with relationships.

One night, Kathy got a phone call from Matthew saying, "Mom, I just rammed my fist and head through a wall and need to go to the ER." Kathy grabbed a cab, picked him up from his friend's house, and took him to the ER. As they sat in the ER waiting, Kathy wondered, but didn't ask, *What memory had been triggered to cause this anger?* She knew he would talk about it when he was ready.

As the parent of two teenagers who had been sexually abused as infants, toddlers, and preschoolers, Kathy's heart was forever broken because every day she knew something could happen to trigger a memory and cause more coping issues for her children.

Both children struggled throughout most of their school years and had a difficult time focusing because of PTSD.

Mary continued to be in and out of therapy since the age of fourteen. Someone should have told Kathy about the continuing and new issues Mary might have so that she could have kept Mary in therapy continuously with the same person instead of moving from job to job and having to find new therapists who always wanted to start at the beginning. What Mary needed was for someone to help her move forward from where she was at each separate moment in time. And even though therapists said they specialized in childhood sexual abuse, most were curious and wanted to hear the details of what happened from the very beginning.

Mary realized she functioned best when she was working with her therapist in Florida, so they moved back so Mary could get the treatment she needed. But even this therapist did not recognize the problems that Mary would still have to deal with as a result of the abuse. After a year, the therapist said Mary had made great progress and could go off to college. But when Mary went off to college, she had blackouts and disassociated, and then she developed an eating disorder and began compulsive shopping and alcohol and drug abuse. No one realized just how much Mary needed to stay at home in a safe environment. When Mary returned to Florida and moved back in with her mother, she told her therapist that it was the first time she felt safe in the last two years, because she continued to disassociate and black out in bad situations.

It is important to note that most nonoffending parents who raise the abused child already feel incompetent for not having been able to prevent the abuse, so this parent depends heavily on the advice and guidance from the therapist treating her child. Therefore, therapists need to recognize the responsibility as well as the consequences of their recommendations to the child and family.

The Twenties

When Matthew was twenty-one, William once again broke the restraining order on Christmas Day by texting Matthew. They wondered how he got Matthew's phone number, but when William said, "I like your work" they realized William had found him on the internet through

Matthew's work website. When Matthew texted back, "who is this" William responded, "your bio Dad." Matthew was shocked and suddenly felt fearful again, knowing this man would never stop stalking him.

The next day, Matthew told Kathy about the text, saying he had not wanted to ruin everyone's Christmas by telling them when it happened. That was Matthew, always so thoughtful and protective when it came to his mom and sister, especially now that he was six foot two and no longer a small child of four years old. Matthew took the lead and told his mom he wanted to make an appointment with the attorney to show him the text so they could document that William once again violated the restraining order. The attorney wrote a letter to William stating his efforts to contact the children were not desired, and even though they were no longer minors, he needed to respect the restraining order, and if he did violate it again, he would be taken back to court. But William had accomplished what he wanted, as now Matthew knew William would be following him through his work website. William was trying to reassert his power over Matthew and cause Matthew to live in fear that William could always find him through his work.

Both children had a lot of difficulty trying to deal with the memories and pain but did not have appropriate coping skills and found alcohol effective in numbing the pain. Although neither Matthew nor Mary ever harmed anyone, they were both arrested once in situations where a memory was triggered that resulted in unsafe behavior and a night in jail even though they had harmed no other person. But their biological father who criminally sexually abused both of them for four years, never did any jail time and has no arrest record because of the mediation and settlements that resulted in closed and nonpublic records of his abuse. Again, what kind of justice is this? These children who had already suffered the most heinous of crimes, also had to endure the trauma of being arrested and taken to jail for being under the influence, even when no one was hurt. No exceptions were made, and no support was offered for the different coping mechanisms/skills that could have helped these children.

Mary had great difficulties with abandonment issues and relationships. When things didn't work out or someone would let her down or leave her or break up with her, she didn't know how to handle it and took everything as rejection. She has suffered alcohol and drug addictions, as well as eating disorders. She found good support from excellent therapists in rehab to help her understand why she turned to alcohol and drugs and how to develop more healthy coping mechanisms. More recently, Mary was the victim of life-threatening domestic violence from an abusive relationship. She has now taken charge or her life, has a therapy/protective dog, and kickboxing for self-defense. She is moving forward, one day at a time.

Matthew has had difficulty focusing and dealing with stressful situations or jobs with male supervisors which is not unusual for survivors suffering PTSD. He has found he is most successful working for himself which is a different kind of stress, but at least he does not have to deal with the conflicts related to power relationships of supervisors. He is learning what works for him, is expanding his profession, and has found someone he can trust because she understands him and expressed her support and love for him by actually hugging him and saying, "I am so sorry this happened to you as tears streamed down her face." With her help, Matthew has recently found a mental health professional he is comfortable working with and is finding therapy to be very helpful. This further documents why mental health support should be provided through decisions made *in the best interest of the child* for victims of childhood sexual abuse *throughout a survivor's life* so this support is always available without additional costs to the survivor.

A Life of Coping—Not Living

Both children have lived a life of coping—always coping with what the abuse to them as an infant, toddler, and preschooler did to the rest of their life. The impact of childhood sexual abuse is far more damaging than most realize.

These children struggle to survive every day because of post-traumatic stress disorder from having been sexually abused at such a young age and having their innocence taken from them in such a heinous way by a trusted parent.

It is important to emphasize that early childhood abuse has serious long-term traumatic consequences for the child. Sexual abuse affects survivors differently at different stages of life as noted in this case study with examples from childhood, teenage years, and into the twenties. When a child is sexually abused by a parent, the physical, emotional, and psychological damage is overwhelming and lasts a lifetime.

Survivors struggle every day. It is important to emphasize the impact of childhood sexual abuse and the related challenges of the children in this case study reflect the same challenges that *every* survivor of childhood sexual abuse faces in some way and to some extent throughout their lives although each one may deal with these challenges in different ways. They learn to cope in whatever way they can. After all, the life they are living is the result of a heinous crime and the related decisions made in the best interest of the child.

The purpose of this book is to raise awareness. Please open your eyes and your hearts and listen to your children.

Summary and Call to Action for Policy Makers, the
Legal Profession, and Mental Health Professionals

The purpose of this book is to promote awareness about the continuing prevalence of childhood sexual abuse and the lifelong impact on victims/survivors. Specifically, it is intended

- to educate all stakeholders and bring to attention the need to believe, support, and improve the lives of survivors of childhood sexual abuse and
- to call for a change in policies and the legal system, in order to support survivors and hold abusers accountable for their actions, regardless of the age of the child.

We need a more just legal system to protect and support victims, along with improved decisions regarding the best interest of the child, including long-term support for mental health and other needs of survivors of this heinous crime.

It is important to emphasize that early childhood sexual abuse has serious long-term traumatic consequences for the child. When a child is sexually abused by a parent or trusted adult, the physical, emotional, and psychological damage is overwhelming and lasts a lifetime.

Children who are sexually abused are more likely to experience various addictions, including alcohol and drugs, eating disorders, and compulsive actions. Further, children who have been sexually abused are more likely to disassociate and black out, have anger issues, have abandonment issues, experience more abusive relationships, and suffer from many other health and behavior problems. As mentioned earlier, an estimated 90 percent of patients who see professional therapists for addiction issues have a known history of some type of abuse.

- Substance abuse, including alcohol, drugs, and food, is a common consequence of early sexual abuse.
- Addictions and obsessive-compulsive behavior are especially common among incest survivors. Chemical use/abuse/addiction serves a survival purpose. It numbs pain and creates a sense of aliveness or excitement for one who may feel "dead" inside.
- Obsessive-compulsive behavior, which is irrational or excessive behavior, provides temporary relief of some perpetual inner struggle.
- Many survivors also have abusive relationships and problems with intimacy.
- Those who were separated from family members as a result of the abuse may experience abandonment issues.
- A majority of children and adolescents who attempt suicide have a history of sexual abuse.

It is critical to make sure all survivors of childhood sexual abuse have access to a mental health professional who specializes in childhood sexual abuse. If there is no treatment, many of these survivors do not see any connection with later experiences of addictions, ongoing abusive relationships, feelings of self-loathing, inability to trust, or problems with intimacy.

The Rights of the Child

All survivors of child sexual abuse deserve the right

- to be heard,
- to be believed,
- to hold their abusers accountable, and
- to receive any needed mental health or other support services at no cost to the survivor.

The time is long overdue to help the many survivors who have suffered from childhood sexual abuse. The pain, anguish, and shattered dreams of so many individuals cannot be left unresolved and forgotten. For those abused by a parent or someone loved and trusted, this unforgiveable, heinous act can cause trauma and issues throughout the child's life.

A call to action is needed for these survivors, to help them throughout their lives. Survivors are everywhere. As mentioned earlier, there are an estimated sixty million survivors of sexual abuse in the United States of which forty million survivors are under the age of thirteen (Merryn 2012). Further, unless changes are made in our legal system, another 400,000 children who are born in the United States will become victims of childhood sexual abuse each year (Townsend and Rheingold 2013). Every eight minutes, Child Protective Services substantiates or finds evidence for a claim of childhood sexual abuse (RAINN, 2018).

The legal system must take responsibility for protecting the rights of children, not only for that moment in time but also for the lifelong consequences of childhood sexual abuse through decisions made in the best interest of the child. It is critical to review the injustice of our legal system through what is and is not rendered through our justice system and to challenge the law as it is written and executed. (Rosenbaum 2004, 2013).

The fact that our legal system is failing our children is of great concern and not acceptable, especially as related to child sexual abuse. These human rights violations affect children and families of every race, religion, education level, income, and profession.

References

Blume, E. Sue. 1990. *Secret Survivors.* New York: Random House.

Bogorad, Barbara. 1998. *Sexual Abuse: Surviving the Pain.* American Academy of Experts in Traumatic Stress, Inc., NY.

Broman-Fulks, J.J., K.J. Ruggiero, R. F. Hanson, D. W. Smith, H. S. Resnick, D. G. Kilpatrick, and B. S. Saunders. 2007. "Sexual Assault Disclosure in Relation to Adolescent Mental Health: Results from the National Survey of Adolescents." *Journal of Clinical Child and Adolescent Psychology* 36 (2): 260–66.

Child Safety Network, 2018. https://www.childrenssafetynetwork.org.

Davis, L. 2008. *The Courage to Heal: A Guide for Women Survivors of Child Sexual Abuse.* William Morrow, NY.

Darkness to Light. 2018. www.d2l.org.

Dube, S. R., R. F. Anda, C. L. Whitfield, D. W. Brown, V. J. Felitti, M. Dong, and W. H. Giles. 2005. "Long-Term Consequences of Childhood Sexual Abuse by Gender of Victim." *American Journal of Preventative Medicine* 28 (5): 430–38.

Engel, Beverly. 2015. *It Wasn't Your Fault*. California: New Harbinger Publications.

Fang, X. et al. 2012. "The Economic Burden of Child Maltreatment in the United States and Implications for Prevention." *Child Abuse and Neglect*, 36.2, 156-165.

Finkelhor, David, Anne Shattuck, Heather A. Turner, and Sherry L. Hamby. 2014. "The Lifetime Prevalence of Child Sexual Abuse and Sexual Assault Assessed in Late Adolescence." *Journal of Adolescent Health* 55:329–33.

Fortin, Jacey. 2018. "Archdiocise in Minnesota Plans to Settle with Abuse Victims for $210 Million" *New York Times*, May 31, 2018. Retrieved from www.nytimes.com/2018/05/31/us/catholic-abuse-settlement-minnesota.html.

The Foundation of Survivors of Abuse. 2018. http://survivingabuse.org.

Jessie. 1991. *Please Tell: A Child's Story about Sexual Abuse*. Hazelden Foundation.

Leeb, R., T. Lewis, A.J. Zolotor. 2011. "A Review of Physical and Mental Health Consequences of Child Abuse and Neglect and Implications for Practice." *American Journal of Lifestyle Medicine*, 5(5).

Merryn, Erin. 2004, 2012. *Stolen Innocence*. Florida: Health Communications Inc.

Moore-Mallinos, Jennifer. 2005. *Do You Have a Secret?* New York: Barron's.

Myers, John E. B. 1997. *A Mother's Nightmare—Incest*. California: Sage Publications.

Rape, Abuse & Incest National Network. 2018. www.rainn.org.

Reeves, Claire. 2003. *Childhood: It Should Not Hurt.* North Carolina: LTI Publishing.

Rosenbaum, Thane. 2005. *The Myth of Moral Justice: Why Our Legal System Fails to Do What's Right.* New York: Harper Perennial.

Rosenbaum, Thane. 2013. *Payback: The Case for Revenge.* University of Chicago Press.

Smith, D., E. J. Letourneau, B. E. Saunders, D. G. Kilpatrick, H. S. Resnick, and C. L. Best. 2000. "Delay in Disclosure of Childhood Rape: Results from a National Survey." *Child Abuse and Neglect* 24:273–87.

Stop It Now! (2013) *Warning Signs in Children and Adolescents of Possible Child Sexual Abuse.* Northampton, MA. www.stopitnow.org.

Townsend, C., A.A. Rheingold. 2013. "Estimating a Child Sexual Abuse Prevalence Rate for Practitioners" *Darkness to Light.* Retrieved from www.d2l.org.

United States Department of Health and Human Services, Administration for Children and Families, Administration on Children, Youth and Families, Children's Bureau. 2012 (2013). Child Maltreatment Survey.

United States Department of Health and Human Services, Administration for Children and Families, Administration on Children, Youth and Families, Children's Bureau. 2013 (2014). Child Maltreatment Survey.

Wachter, Oralee. 1983. *No More Secrets for Me.* New York: ODN Productions.

Waldrop A. E., R. F. Hanson, H. S. Resnick, D. G. Kilpatrick, A. E. Naugle, and B. E. Saunders. 2007. "Risk Factors for Suicidal Behaviors among a National Sample of Adolescents: Implications for Prevention." *Journal of Traumatic Stress* 20:869–79.

Whitfield, Charles L. 2006. *Healing the Child Within*. Florida: Health Communications Inc.

Yamamoto, DeAnn. 2015. *The Advocate's Guide: Working with Parents of Children Who Have Been Sexually Assaulted*. National Sexual Violence Resource Center. www.nsvrc.org.

Resources

- RAINN (Rape, Abuse & Incest National Network) is the nation's largest anti-sexual-violence organization. RAINN created and operates the National Sexual Assault Hotline. That phone number is 1-800-656-4673 (1-800-656-HOPE). This hotline is in partnership with more than a thousand local sexual assault service providers across the country. RAINN also supports programs to prevent sexual violence, to help survivors, and to ensure that perpetrators are brought to justice. Their website is www.rainn.org. The following resources can be found on (and are copied from) their website.

  - **National Child Abuse Hotline**: They can provide local referrals for services. A centralized call center provides the caller with the option of talking to a counselor. They are also connected to a language line that can provide service in over 140 languages. Hotline: 800.4.A.CHILD (422.2253)
  - **Darkness to Light**: They provide crisis intervention and referral services to children

or people affected by sexual abuse of children. Hotline calls are automatically routed to a local center. Helpline: 866.FOR.LIGHT (367.5444)

- **Cyber Tipline**: This Tipline is operated by the **National Center for Missing and Exploited Children**. Can be used to communicate information to the authorities about child pornography or child sex trafficking. Hotline: 800.THE.LOST (843.5678)
- **National Children's Alliance**: This organization represents the national network of Child Advocacy Centers (CAC). CACs are a multidisciplinary team of law enforcement, mental and physical health practitioners who investigate instances of child physical and sexual abuse. Their website explains the process and has a directory according to geographic location.
- **Stop It Now**: Provides information to victims and parents/relatives/friends of child sexual abuse. The site also has resources for offender treatment as well as information on recognizing the signs of child sexual abuse. Hotline: 888-PREVENT (773.8368)
- **Justice for Children**: Provides a full range of advocacy services for abused and neglected children.

- National Sexual Violence Resource Center (www. nsvrc.org) has published a very helpful document: "The Advocate's Guide: Working with Parents of

Children Who Have Been Sexually Assaulted"
(Yamamota 2015). www.nsvrc.org/publications/
nsvrc-publications-guides/advocates-working-
parents-children-who-have-been-sexually-assaulted.

CPSIA information can be obtained
at www.ICGtesting.com
Printed in the USA
BVHW07s0436050918
526542BV00001BA/45/P

9 781532 054952